SUICIDE AND GRIEF

The Quiet Despair of Grief

It was like walking down a hallway with about forty doors, and never being able to find a door that's open. It was just a quiet, black, sick feeling. And you wanted to find a door that's open, or some outlet, or some escape, and no matter what you did the door wouldn't open. I mean you'd get out with friends or whatever, but it lives with you.

—From the author's interview with
a grieving widow.

SUICIDE AND GRIEF

by HOWARD W. STONE

Fortress Press
Philadelphia

Library of Congress Catalog Card Number 70–171506

ISBN 0–8006–1402–x

3095H72   Printed in the United States of America   1-1402

To my wife
Karen

CONTENTS

PREFACE

This book has a specific focus in mind—the grief reaction which occurs after a suicide is committed. At the same time I believe it will also serve an additional purpose: it will inform the reader about suicide in general and give him information concerning the typical grief reaction which occurs after a non-suicide death. The conclusions and suggestions herein are based on the results of a research project recently completed in Los Angeles, comparing the grief responses of suicide and non-suicide surviving spouses. The book attempts to inform the reader of the typical dynamics that occur in a suicide grief as well as give him some clues as to how to counsel the survivor.

I have consciously directed this book primarily to the minister—especially the parish minister, who works on the front lines with suicide and grief. My reason is that I too am a minister, and I asked some of the same questions asked in this book when I first began ministering to people with problems of living. I was not able to find answers to these questions and therefore discovered the need for such a book. The book has been written so that laymen in the church, who as a part of the "priesthood of all believers" performing an essential ministry to the bereaved, can read it as well. As an aid in understanding this book, the reader should familiarize himself with the terms which are defined and discussed in the Glossary.

It is my hope, furthermore, that *Suicide and Grief* will also reach mental health professionals specializing in the fields of suicide and grief, who will be particularly interested in the statistical findings of the research which are presented.

I acknowledge with gratitude the help I have received from many quarters in the completion of the research and the book. I am indebted to the Lutheran Brotherhood Insurance Company for their generosity in providing the research grant which funded the study.

Preface

I thank Howard Clinebell, Frank Kimper, Paul Irwin, and Paul Pretzel, whose criticism and comments helped shape the form which the research was to take. I also wish to thank the staff of the Suicide Prevention Center of Los Angeles, and especially Drs. Pretzel, Brown, Peck, and Farberow, for their help in developing and carrying out the research. I appreciated the willingness of LeRoy Aden and Martin Roth to read the manuscript and give their comments and criticisms. And I am grateful to my students at the Philadelphia Lutheran Theological Seminary who have helped me clarify my thinking in the area of crisis intervention. Finally I wish to express my gratitude to my wife Karen, for her patience, understanding, and help during all phases of the research and the writing of the book.

1. A GENERIC APPROACH TO SUICIDE AND GRIEF

A Case of Grief in the Family

Bob,

I love you very much and I'm sorry. I just can't go on living the way I have. Life has nothing left to offer me. Give my love to the children. Please forgive me.

Alice[1]

Bob Dickinson found this slightly crumpled note waiting for him when he arrived home. He had gone to work early Friday morning, about 5:00 A.M., to catch up on some paper work. Before leaving he told his wife, who was still in bed, that he would contact the new doctor they had decided on seeing only the day before.

Alice was in the "change of life," as Bob described it. He said it had been rough for her. She had also been troubled by some stomach problems—he called it "spastic something-or-other." She had some trouble sleeping but it had not caused her to miss much work. (She was a secretary for a large Los Angeles firm.) Both Bob and Alice felt their present doctor wasn't doing all he could for her, and they had decided to see a new doctor in Glendale.

About 8:30 A.M. that Friday, Bob's twenty-year-old daughter drove to his office to tell him that Alice had shot herself.

Bob, in his forties, had been married to Alice for twenty-one years. He described the marriage as a "fairly close" one. "We had differences, but . . . we never had any fights or anything, because . . . she wasn't the type and I wasn't the type. . . ." They did everything together; he said he had not been separated from Alice more than two or three days at a time in their entire marriage. Although they talked with each other, he felt he had not listened to her enough—especially in the last months when she was struggling with menopause. She had never been one to talk about how she felt and he had been so busy at work that he hadn't taken much time to ask her about things.

When Bob's daughter told him that Alice had shot herself, he was stunned. When he arrived home he learned that she had been with the children, then left them and went into her bedroom, and shot herself through the temple. She was dead on arrival at the hospital. Now, at home, Bob began to feel the crushing force of his grief. He had not expected this; she had never (to his knowledge) talked about committing suicide.

Why did she do it? What could he have done to stop it? What was he, a father of four children from ages eleven to twenty, to do now? Should he tell his friends that she had committed suicide, or say it was an accident? Like the whirlpools at the bottom of a waterfall, thousands of unanswered questions began swirling in his head.

Suicide Grief Reaction

The dilemma we face in dealing with suicide has become increasingly evident to ministers, mental health professionals, and the general public. In the last ten to fifteen years the government and private foundations have funded suicide prevention centers across the United States in an endeavor to curtail suicides.

The uneasiness that many people feel when confronted with the task of helping the bereaved is also well known. Many ministers are not satisfied with how they handle the grief period and the funeral. When the two emotionally charged issues of suicide and grief are combined, the minister faces an extremely difficult situation of pastoral care. It is to this situation that this book addresses itself.

Mental health professionals have recently sought more information on the dynamics of suicide survivors. In February of 1970 the National Institute of Mental Health held a symposium in Phoenix which focused on what people in the field of suicidology should be doing in the new decade. Three of the six position papers presented at this conference indicated a need for a greater knowledge concerning families of completed suicides, the grief of suicide survivors, and how to effectively help these families. The paper by Ronald W. Maris indicated the need for studying and reconstructing the life histories and situational components of completed suicides.[2] Norman Farberow's paper on research in suicide stated, ". . . clergymen could use such information [about deatth and grief] in working with families where suicide, death or suicidal behavior has occurred."[3] Richard K. McGee, in another paper, expressed his belief that such information can be used to help prevent future suicides.[4]

Recently Gene W. Brokopp, in discussing what people in the field of suicide will be doing in the present decade, made seven predictions. One is that more effort will be focused on the families of individuals who have committed suicide.

> We now recognize that a person who makes a suicide attempt or who commits suicide . . . is affected in his act by those who surround him and that he deeply affects them. When, for example, suicide does take place, the scars that it leaves in the family and significant friends are profound and require the assistance of people who are specifically trained in work in this type of situation.[5]

Cain and Fast, who are working in the area of the effect of suicide on the survivors, state:

> . . . the implicit interpersonal tugs and pulls of the suicidal person's general pre-suicidal behavior and ultimate suicidal act have profound effects upon his actual external objects—effects lasting long after the suicide act—which virtually cry out for study and intervention.[6]

All realize that the family of an individual who commits suicide has a high suicide risk and needs help of some sort. Yet for some reason little research has been done on the grief responses of suicide survivors. The great bulk of the work in this area has been in the form of "psychological autopsies"[7] which are done fairly soon after the death, studies of children who have lost a parent by suicide, or studies by psychotherapists of their clients who have lost parents or spouses years earlier by suicide.

Furthermore, these studies have been made by suicidologists, psychiatrists, and psychologists; little has been done by ministers.[8] This lack of work by theologically trained pastoral counselors is quite surprising since suicide, death, and grief involve deep religious questions. They are part of the "warp and woof" of the ministerial experience.

3

Purpose of the Book

The purpose of this book, then, is to provide the reader with information concerning both the basic dynamics of grief, how the suicide and non-suicide grief are both similar and different, and also to suggest some ways in which the minister can aid both suicide and non-suicide survivors during difficult periods of their grief. After the introduction and a background chapter on the topics of suicide and grief in general, the two main thrusts of the book will be: (a) to explain the dynamics of grief after a completed suicide, and (b) to suggest some ways of ministering to the survivors. Chapters 3 and 4 will discuss the dynamics of grief, comparing suicide grief with non-suicide grief reactions. Chapters 5 and 6 will focus on the pastoral care and counseling of the suicide survivors. Appendices are included at the end to explain the way that the research for the book was done. They include tables of some of the research findings.

Emphasizing certain dynamics which generally occur within a specific type of crisis, as well as suggesting specific ways in which this particular type of crisis can be dealt with, has been referred to in crisis intervention theory as the "generic approach."[9] Several excellent examples of the use of this approach can be found in the work of Gerald Caplan and Erich Lindemann. The central reasoning for the generic approach is that for each crisis, e.g., death, divorce, premature birth, etc., there are definite identifiable patterns (dynamics) which generally occur. The first person to note this occurrence was Lindemann in his classic work on grief among families of those who died in the Coconut Grove fire.[10] He showed quite clearly that the survivors of death go through a well-defined process in resolving their loss. Lindemann called it "grief work." A more detailed discussion is included in the second chapter.

The generic approach does not try to glean the specific psychodynamics of a particular individual's grief, but rather focuses on the course which a particular type of crisis usually follows, and on a method of intervention[11] that will aid the individual in having a more adaptive resolution of the crisis. Thus, in the case of the grief reaction to a suicide, the minister needs to be aware of the specific course that this special grief usually takes. He also needs to know of pastoral care and counseling approaches that are particularly effective in resolving this grief in an adaptive way. It is hoped that the minister will go beyond the generic approach to an individually tailored approach, taking into consideration not only the particular characteristics and natural course of the suicidal grief, but also how it expresses itself within a particular person's own personality structure, his typical emotional dynamics, his problem areas, etc.

Suicide Grief and Preventative Pastoral Care

In times of emotional stress people turn to the minister more than to any other professional person. As a result of its survey in 1960, the Joint Commission on Mental Illness and Health found that of the professional persons to whom people turn in times of emotional stress, about 42% consult clergymen, 29% go for help to physicians, only 19% consult psychiatrists or psychologists, and 10% go to social agencies or clinics. The minister is traditionally the person to whom people go in time of death. The opportunity is usually there for the clergy and the people of God to prevent or modify a potentially destructive grief reaction. Glenn E. Whitlock identifies the carrying out of this function as preventative pastoral care.[12]

Preventative pastoral care focuses on (1) reducing the incidence of pastoral care problems, (2) reducing the duration of such problems, and (3) reducing the residual impairment that may result from these problems.

From the standpoint of preventative pastoral care, the minister may not only have the first opportunity to help members of a family after a suicidal death, but he may also have more chance to help them because of a previously established relationship.

A pastor trained in the understanding of the psychodynamics of human behavior will be sensitive to the "danger signals" and the psychological "tilts" which may be observed in individuals and families in varying degrees of emotional stress.[13]

NOTES

1. Names, places, and certain details have been changed in the cases referred to in this book. The suicide note is hypothetical.

2. Ronald W. Maris et al., "Education and Training in Suicidology for the Seventies" (Paper delivered at the Phoenix conference of the National Institute of Mental Health: "Suicide in the Seventies," 1970), p. 13.

3. Norman Farberow, "Research in Suicide" (Paper delivered at the Phoenix conference of the NIMH: "Suicide in the Seventies," 1970), p. 45.

4. Richard K. McGee, "The Delivery of Suicide Prevention Services" (Paper presented at the Phoenix conference of the NIMH: "Suicide in the Seventies," 1970), pp. 6–7.

5. Gene W. Brokopp, "Seven Predictions for Suicide Prevention in the Seventies," *Crisis Intervention* II:1 (1970): 7.

6. Albert C. Cain and Irene Fast, "The Legacy of Suicide: Observations on the Pathogenic Impact of Suicide Upon Marital Partners," *Psychiatry* XXIX:4 (1966): 407.

7. The psychological autopsy is an interdisciplinary method of research which attempts to evaluate the preterminal and terminal phases of life of a recently deceased individual, and to determine the role of psychological factors in his death. It is used in some cities to determine whether or not an undetermined death is a suicide.

8. There are exceptions, such as Paul Pretzel's work in suicide.

9. See especially Gerald F. Jacobsen, Martin Strickler, and Wilbur E. Morley, "Generic and Individual Approaches to Crisis Intervention," *American Journal of Public Health* LVIII:2 (February, 1968): 340–41; and Wilbur E. Morley, "Theory of Crisis Intervention," *Pastoral Psychology* XXI:203 (April, 1970): 17–18.

10. Erich Lindemann, "Symptomatology and Management of Acute Grief," *Pastoral Psychology* XIV:36 (September, 1963): 8–18.

11. Or crisis intervention; see definition in Glossary.

12. Glenn E. Whitlock, "Pastoral Psychology and Preventive Psychiatry," *Pastoral Psychology* XXI:203 (April, 1970): 9–13.

13. Ibid., p. 12.

2. UNDERSTANDING GRIEF
   AND SUICIDE

The minister who does counseling will perhaps never have a lot of practice in counseling suicide survivors. Many, many more people will come to him with their grief after a loved one has died from a long illness, or a heart attack, or an accident. And he will no doubt have to deal with a greater number of threatened suicides, or even attempted suicides, because many more people talk about committing suicide than actually complete the act. A knowledge about grief in general, and suicide in particular, is essential to ministering in these situations.

Grief Responses

Authors in the field of pastoral care and counseling have been interested in grief for a number of years. Most of the work in pastoral counseling, as in psychiatry and psychology, has operated from a psychoanalytic framework; the attempt in the present work is to be more eclectic from the standpoint of psychological theory. Furthermore, most work in pastoral counseling has studied individuals who were having psychological difficulty with their grief and came for counseling; whereas the sample for the present study is a normal rather than pathological population.

Two writers who have probably done the most work on grief in the field of pastoral care are Paul Irion and Edgar Jackson (their books are listed in the Bibliography). David K. Switzer, a recent author in the field of pastoral care, has written a good survey of different approaches to grief, *The Dynamics of Grief*.

Lindemann's classic article on the management of grief, for which he studied the survivors of the famed Coconut Grove fire, is still valuable. Lindemann differentiates between normal and morbid grief

7

ₙe disruptions of the normal grief reaction which make
one are caused by either a delay in the beginning of the
ₗstorted reaction, i.e., one that is characterized by any of
ₙg: (1) overactivity without a sense of loss; (2) the ac-
f symptoms belonging to the last illness of the deceased;
(3) a recognized medical disease (such as ulcerative colitis or
asthma); (4) alteration in relationships with friends and relatives;
(5) furious hostility; (6) a lasting loss of patterns of social interac-
tion; (7) a large amount of activities that are detrimental to the
survivor's own social or economic existence; and (8) agitated depression.[1]

Clayton, Desmarais, and Winokur's study of normal bereavement
is probably the best work on normal grief from an empirical standpoint. They interviewed relatives of a deceased person to determine
their common symptoms of grief. Only three symptoms occurred in
over half of the subjects: depression, sleep disturbance, and crying.
In a follow-up visit within three months of the death they found
81% of the bereaved improved, i.e., experienced a reduction in their
symptoms; 15% felt better in spite of the symptoms still existing;
and only 4% were worse.[2]

Marris's book, *Widows and Their Families,* reports his 1958 study
on the adjustment of London widows to their husbands' death. Although the research methods leave something to be desired, it was
one of the first attempts by a researcher to make a statistical study.
Marris lists five reactions which occurred in most of his subjects:
(1) lasting deterioration in health; (2) difficulty in sleeping; (3)
loss of contact with reality; (4) withdrawal; and (5) hostility.[3] Unfortunately, the use of nonsystematic interviews in both Marris's
and Lindemann's studies makes their findings difficult to evaluate.

Finally, a recent development in the study of death and especially
of suicide is the psychological autopsy.[4] Several articles have been
written describing it.[5] As a method of studying the events preceding
a death, the psychological autopsy has improved suicide reporting. It
was originated by Theodore Curphey who at the time was Chief
Medical Examiner-Coroner of Los Angeles County. (Farberow and
Shneidman were also instrumental in its development.) Since suicidal individuals usually leave clues to their intentions, "death in-
vestigative teams" are frequently able to uncover the true cause of
death.

New figures

The psychological autopsy has also been used to study the final events preceding a death for the purpose of better understanding the motives which led to suicide. Farberow and Simon, in "A Suicide Tale of Two Cities: An Intercultural Study," use the psychological autopsy to study the dynamics which led to actual suicides in Vienna and Los Angeles. While this study does not deal directly with grief responses, it yields some interesting data on the cause of suicide. It suggests that the stresses (e.g., a recent loss, illness, physical and emotional exhaustion, etc.) which lead to suicide are fairly universal. Generally there was an absence of social cohesion and communication, even in subjects who had families. "It was striking to note how little spouses knew about the thoughts, hopes, aspirations and problems of their partners."[6]

The Patterns of Suicide

Each year at least twenty thousand suicides are recorded in the United States, although the actual figure may be twice that. Eight times as many people attempt suicide in a year. The death rate by suicide is greater than by tuberculosis, leukemia, rheumatic fever, ulcers, or homicide (taken individually). In the following pages I hope to condense some of what we now know about suicide, but the reader should not draw the conclusion that our information about suicide is definitive and complete. The study of suicide is in its infancy and we still have much to learn.

Why does a person commit suicide? In *The Cry for Help*, seven theoretical bases for understanding suicide are suggested, from the Freudian to the nondirective points of view. In summarizing these different points of view, Farberow sees five significant dynamics.[7]

1. The person who is suicidal is a *dependent* person. Frequently he has been involved in a "sticky" symbiotic relationship, and when this relationship is threatened or lost he develops suicidal impulses.

2. The second dynamic, *aggression and hostility,* serves three motives: coercive, retaliatory, and expiatory. Suicide can be a method of hurting others by hurting oneself, or a way in which the individual attempts to manipulate others by his act or threatened act. In this way it is a form of psychological blackmail in which the suicidal individual feels he can get what he wants. It can also be acted-out self-hatred, or expiation for real or imagined guilt.

9

3. As mentioned above the *guilt* dynamic in suicide can serve as the motivation for an expiatory act of suicide. Suicide thus becomes self-inflicted punishment for unacceptable (usually angry) feelings toward someone who has disappointed the individual.

4. Most authors on suicide indicate that *anxiety* is an important element in suicide. When tension builds to unacceptably high levels in an individual, suicide becomes an escape. Severe anxiety occurs when a person feels everything in life is chaotic and indeterminate. This involves a feeling of lack of control and suicide is one way that the individual can control something—his own death.

5. The fifth dynamic is *adaption*. Theorists on suicide agree that an individual does not have to be psychotic or hopelessly neurotic to commit suicide. Suicide can be a mentally healthy individual's adaptation to his particular situation. So for the captain who goes down with his ship, or the individual with a fatal disease who is suffering deeply, committing suicide is a way of adapting to his environment. Ethically we may disagree with this act of suicide but we cannot pass it off as an act "done by a psychotic who didn't know what he was doing."

It should be noted that depression or agitated depression are not included in Farberow's list. Not all suicidal individuals are depressed or in a state of agitated depression; it is a fairly common dynamic but not at all universal.

Most suicidal activity is interpersonal in nature, i.e., it is done in relation to other people. Several authors have attempted to study the interpersonal dynamics of a suicide situation.[8] One of the most interesting studies, by Michael Peck of the Los Angeles Suicide Prevention Center, was of the "double bind" among married couples and families in which one of the individuals is suicidal. Communication between people occurs at two levels—verbal and nonverbal. When an individual gives one verbal message and a different nonverbal one, this is what Peck calls double bind communication. He found that about 25% of couples and families where one member is suicidal communicate in such a way. He lists the following characteristics of the double bind communicator:

> His martyr-like determination to accept whatever occurs within the family as part of his burden in a difficult life; his subsequent denial that difficulties are, in fact, present and assertion that everything happens for the best; or all will turn out well in the long run. His

vociferous denial that he's conflicted about anything important, and that he has any feelings of anger or resentment toward his spouse or children, and his maintenance of this position through an over-identification with the role of mother, father, husband or wife. Finally, a strong verbal assertion of his strength which he equates with his family being dependent upon him, in various ways, but his not being dependent on them or anyone for that matter.[9]

On the other hand, the suicidal individual is very dependent and demanding. He sees himself as helpless, emotionally erratic, and as a failure who cannot fulfill the expectations of others. Difficulties begin when the potentially suicidal person tries to communicate to his pseudocompetent, pseudodominant mate his feelings of failure. These feelings are not accepted and the dependent spouse is assured verbally that everything is all right. At the same time the dominant spouse communicates nonverbally his uncertainty that all is in fact well; the dependent spouse picks up this uncertainty, and he is even more confused about how his spouse feels about him. Then, to quote Peck, the dependent-suicidal individual

> . . . enters into his suicidal actions as an attempt to comment on the denial and duplicity inherent in his spouse's message and to force his spouse to take a stand in relation to him. Until this behavior occurs it seems that the two persons failed to communicate directly with each other, but rather they relate to their projections, wishes or ideas about the other. Under these circumstances a fusion relationship develops and continues whereby each person avoids establishing himself as an independent person, but rather views himself as a part of the other. The dominant member maintains a fantasy of being the good parent whose child is a symbiotic part of him. The dependent partner maintains a fantasy of the needy-demanding infant who wishes to have a good parent to rely upon to gratify his needs, but is always disappointed. They manage to maintain this unrealistic fusion by a pattern of communication which may be called mutual double binding.[10]

It needs to be emphasized that only 25% of the individuals researched fit into this category. There is no one specific situation which always produces potentially suicidal individuals. However, suicide does frequently occur in highly interpersonal situations, which is an important fact for one concerned with the survivor's grief. It is in the interpersonal, double bind relationship that potentially unadaptive grief reactions may occur.

A final note about the interpersonal aspects of suicide. In the research for this book three questions were asked to discern the spouse's perception of the quality of the marriage at the time of death:

(5) Our marriage at the time of death was going "downhill."

(12) I don't completely understand why, but in the last few months before the death of my spouse, we argued and verbally fought a lot.

(15) My spouse hardly ever confided in me.

The first two questions revealed a significant difference between suicide and non-suicide spouses.[11] The suicide spouses generally did not feel their marriage had been as good at the time of death as the non-suicide spouses. Because of the kind of statistical test which was used, the factors of guilt and feelings about the marriage relationship cannot be considered to be highly related. The suicide spouse's poorer evaluation of the marriage relationship before death is probably not due in any great degree to the guilt he feels.

The signs that an individual may be thinking of committing suicide are not always difficult to discern, especially once the process has begun. About 80% of those who commit suicide give definite warnings of their intentions. Many people do not take these warnings seriously, either because they are afraid or because they do not feel they are important. The suicidal person will typically manifest many of the following clues to his intentions:[12]

a. Ambivalence. The suicidal individual has mixed feelings about committing suicide ("to be or not to be"). For example, a thirty-five-year-old housewife ingests a lethal dose of barbiturates, but then asks to be rescued (indirectly) by calling a friend "to say good-bye." If suicidal individuals did not have this ambivalence about dying, suicide prevention would be almost impossible.

b. Crisis. The suicidal person is generally in a state of crisis, often stimulated by a loss or threatened loss.[13] An intense experience pressures the individual toward some form of resolution—either adaptive or unadaptive. Something has to change to resolve the crisis, and a few people see suicide as a way out.

c. Feelings of futility. The suicidal individual feels pressed to drastic measures by his situation. He feels helpless to handle it and so hopeless that he will consider taking his own life.

d. Exhaustion. The suicidal individual usually is physically or emotionally exhausted and frequently both. So much of his energy is devoted to his own problems that he has difficulty doing even routine tasks without great effort.

e. Communication. The process of preparing to kill oneself is a last-ditch effort to communicate to others one's desperation. It is a cry for help. Statements such as "I'm tired of life" and "I'm going to end it all" are verbal communications. Nonverbal gestures such as buying a gun or giving away prized possessions are also meant to communicate the individual's intentions.

f. Unresolved feelings. The suicidal individual frequently has strong unrelieved feelings of depression, guilt, anxiety or hostility.

g. Disruption in life. Frequently he feels he is living a life of chaos and disorganization. Nothing can be counted on; there is little security.

h. Mood swings. Many times a suicidal person has wide mood swings from agitation to withdrawal. This can be a sign of an agitated depression.

i. Cognitive constriction. The person who is suicidal has difficulty discerning the various alternatives which are open to him. His thinking is so polarized that he may say, "Either I must continue to live in the hell I am in now, or I must commit suicide." He does not see other possibilities he can choose.

j. Interest loss. Loss of interest in an accustomed and enjoyed activity (work, recreation, sex) is a very important nonverbal clue that a person is contemplating suicide.

k. Physical distress and psychosomatic symptoms. The final clue to a potential suicide is if the person experiences anxiety attacks, sleep disturbance, and psychosomatic symptoms. These are behavioral indicators that he is struggling with emotional problems and may have suicide thoughts.

All of the above are signs that a person may be suicidal. They are not all present in every case, nor is any one sign a definite clue that a person is suicidal. They can serve as warning flags to the minister, signaling that he needs to become rapidly involved with the individual to determine if he really is suicidal.

The Handling of a Suicide Crisis

The focus of this book is upon the pastoral care of the survivors after a suicide is committed; but how does one handle the suicide crisis itself? How do you deal with the phone call at 3:00 A.M. from a parishioner who is estranged from her husband and says she is going to take some sleeping pills? How seriously do you take the comment of a young mother of two children, "I sometimes get so exhausted taking care of the kids and all that I think it would be easier to end it all"?[14]

The Suicide Prevention Center in Los Angeles has developed guidelines for the effective handling of a suicide crisis.[15] I have modified and added to these guidelines, and suggest a four-point model of pastoral intervention. There are two main considerations in dealing with the suicidal individual: first, the necessity of rapidly developing a counseling relationship, and second, the necessity of evaluating the lethality of the suicide threat. In Chapter 5 a more extensive treatment will be given to the method of crisis intervention counseling. Below are four major goals that need to be accomplished in dealing with the suicidal individual.

1. *Rapidly develop a relationship* with the individual (if you have not already). You as the minister need to be calm, patient, interested, hopeful, and knowledgeable. You need to communicate to the suicidal individual a positive concern and a feeling that you can and will help, not "I don't know what to do." It is best to talk to him without a high level of anxiety. Speak calmly, and do not be overtaken by his own anxiety. You will want to communicate by your attitude that he has done the right thing in coming to you for help. He may see you as his last hope, and will probably be testing you to see if you are competent and can be trusted. If he is able to discern that you are a relaxed, caring, competent individual, you are solving one of his most pressing problems. You also need to be able to accept without challenge or criticism what he has to say. While you are developing the relationship, at the beginning your goal is to obtain information that can be used in the evaluation of the lethality of the suicide threat. When you ask questions of the individual it is best to be direct and specific. For example, "How do you plan on committing suicide?" "Do you have any guns or pills?" "Do you have a gun with you? Is it near you? Is it in your hand? Is it loaded?"

When the person mentions to you that he wants to commit suicide, he is asking for help. He is willing to talk about it, or he would never have mentioned it. Many times suicidal impulses are felt as uncontrollable feelings which frighten the individual. He wants to talk with

14

someone who is self-assured and not frightened away by these feelings.

2. *Focus the problem.* The suicidal individual and other people in crisis frequently feel a great sense of confusion in their lives. A person considering suicide may not know what is going on—the world has fallen apart for him and he is like a little lost boy. Another individual may know very specifically what the crisis is but not know how to cope with it. The first person becomes lost in a myriad of details and is unclear about his problem. In his case it is best not to just sit back and listen to all of the details; it is wise for the minister *person* fairly soon to slice in and cut out the extraneous details which cloud the issue. The problem needs to be focused. Sometimes the individual does not know why he feels suicidal, even though, for example, he may have recently found that he has terminal cancer. The second individual has a clear focus but has exhausted all the alternatives. Here you as a reasonably objective outsider can help him evaluate different alternatives of action and provide additional suggestions. This helps break the cognitive constriction he is experiencing and leads toward a more responsible decision.

3. *Assess the lethality of the suicide impulses and the personal resources of the individual.* The assessment of the suicide potential is what makes this model of counseling unique in comparison to other methods of crisis intervention counseling. Nine basic criteria need to be evaluated. I am not suggesting that you use these criteria as a checklist, but that you internalize them and find the answers informally but directly as you talk with the suicidal individual. If you need help in your evaluation of the lethality of the suicide threat, call the local suicide prevention center or a counselor or therapist who has specialized in suicide. The following are the criteria for judging suicide lethality:

a. Age and sex. About 60% of all completed suicides are men, yet women attempt suicide more than men. Thus a man's suicide threat is more dangerous than a woman's. With men especially, the threat of suicide increases in lethality with age. A recently retired man of 65 who says life no longer has any meaning for him must be taken very seriously. While the suicide index (the number of individuals per 100,000 who commit suicide each year) for men aged 15–24 is 7.4, the index at 64–75 years is 45.5—a dramatic difference. Older men commit suicide most frequently; teen-age girls the least.

(Yet teen-age girls do commit suicide; _all_ talk of suicide must be taken seriously.)

b. The suicide plan. This is the most important criterion. You need to ask if he has decided how he wants to commit suicide. What you want to know is how specific is the plan, how lethal is the method, and how available are the means. The success ratio of wrist slitting is small; a gun is pretty successful. Some pills are more lethal than others, and if the individual is taking tranquilizing drugs prescribed by an M.D., let the physician know so he can prescribe drugs that are not very lethal (you have to take bottles and bottles of some compounds before you can kill yourself).

In general, an individual who has a very specific plan, has spent a good amount of time thinking about how he is going to do it, has a lethal method like hanging or shooting, and has means readily available, is a very serious suicide risk.

c. Stress. Typically a serious suicide threat occurs while an individual is in crisis, usually precipitated by a loss or threatened loss such as death, loss of job, divorce or separation, incapacitating accident or illness, etc. Sometimes merely change, such as promotion to a management position or a success of some other sort, can raise anxieties and cause stress. An example is a lathe operator who did such an excellent job that he was promoted to foreman and soon came into counseling feeling very depressed. He could not cope with the pressure of being in charge of other people and meeting quotas. This is an example of how stress must be evaluated in the client's eyes and not in the counselor's. What may be perceived as a small promotion to the minister can be a matter of life or death to the parishioner.

A good rule of thumb concerning stress is that if the stress as well as the plan and the symptoms are severe, then a very active response is required of the minister. On the other hand, if the stress does not appear to be severe, then the minister either does not have the complete story or he is dealing with a chronically unstable individual. Such a person needs to be reminded of the previous crises he has weathered—perhaps not well, but at least survived—and he needs to be assured that he will be helped to deal with his present problem.

d. Symptoms. An individual does not have to be depressed to commit suicide; it can happen as a result of several different emotional states: _Depressive_ states—not every depressive commits suicide, but

16

depressive individuals do have a moderately high suicide potential. *Psychotic* states—suicide among psychotics is fairly high. *Borderline* psychotic—this is frequently indicated by a very bizarre suicide plan. *Agitated* states—if the individual shows a lot of tension and is constantly moving, can't sit still, his condition is very serious. The most serious emotional state is the agitated depressive state. Suicide among individuals who are depressed generally occurs as they are beginning to come out of the depression. At the bottom they lack the ego strength to do it, but when they are feeling better they can sum up the determination to complete the act. Alcoholics and homosexuals or other sexual deviates have high suicide rates, as do drug users, in comparison with the general populace.

e. Meaning and religious involvement. It was found in the present study as well as in others that individuals who are involved in the church, have fairly strong religious beliefs, and have a purpose in life are immunized to some extent from becoming suicidal. It is therefore important to find out if the person is involved regularly with a church or some religious group and if he has a relationship with a pastor. It is also good to know what, if anything, is giving him meaning in life. If he is neither influenced by nor committed to anything, he is bereft of this form of social constraint against suicide; he is freer to complete the act. However, highly religious individuals also commit suicide.

f. Resources.[16] What can friends, relatives, physicians, social workers, ministers, and fellow workers do to help the suicidal individual during his crisis? It is necessary to evaluate which of these resources can give him support. When I ask people about resources at their disposal, some reply, "None, nobody cares." The counselor should not at first take this literally because there are often more people who care than the individual realizes. The task of the minister then is to discern which of these resources are helpful in aiding the individual in his suicidal crisis or which may be detrimental.

If the suicidal client has already been in counseling with someone else, it is good to transfer him back to the original counselor if possible. I frequently find it helpful to call the counselor (with the individual's permission) and tell him about the suicide threat. This often helps cut through waiting lists and opens up an appointment.

A valuable resource for both the minister and the suicidal individual is a local suicide prevention or crisis center. However, the

17

minister should be aware of the quality of the local center. Recently some have been started on a shoestring by well-meaning individuals who have not been adequately trained and cannot give sound consultation. There are many competent suicide prevention centers which can be of great help throughout the country. Most, however, are located in large cities.

It is generally best for both the minister and the person coming to him for help to be very open with outside people about suicidal feelings. This is valuable because it gives the suicidal individual the feeling he lacks: that others are concerned about him and ready to help. It is valuable for the minister because it helps to share the responsibility of the suicide potential with others. Often, I have found, with a little encouragement the individual is willing to share his feelings with others. Sometimes I will ask him to tell certain people about his problems; in other cases where the individual seems more seriously suicidal and immobilized I myself will call some of his resource persons and tell them he is considering suicide. If a situation arose where a person seemed very suicidal but did not want me to tell anyone, I would consider doing it anyway if I felt I could prevent him from committing suicide.

g. Life-style. Two important aspects need to be discerned regarding life-style—whether or not the life-style of the individual is stable, and whether the suicide idea is acute or chronic. A stable personality can be determined by behavioral indicators such as consistent work history, stable marriage and family relations, and an absence of suicidal activity in the past. The unstable personality may exhibit any of the following: chronic alcoholism, going from job to job, borderline psychosis, character disorder, a series of crises which never seem to be resolved well. Acute suicidal gestures are found in both stable and unstable personalities, while chronic suicide threats occur only among unstable personalities.

h. Communication. The minister needs to find out if the person threatening suicide is communicating with other people, and what has been his style of communication. This is vital because if he is *not* communicating with others it can be a sign that he has given up hope and will at least attempt suicide. The style of communication is also important. Whether the communication is open and direct, or vague and indirect, is important, as well as whether the communication is verbal or nonverbal. The college student who gave away his most prized possessions and a week later committed suicide is an example of an indirect nonverbal communication. This type of communication is difficult to discern and rarely reaches the attention of the mental health professional, unless the individual has been in counseling for some time. Thus it is up to the family and key resource people like the minister to read the intent behind such gestures. One of the pastor's main tasks is to clarify the indirect and nonverbal communication for those who are closely involved with the individual. It is important that the individual know where he can turn if he feels suicidal again. At first the counselor may be the only person he will trust with his feelings.

i. *Medical record.* The minister should know if the suicidal individual has an impending or has had a recent operation, or a chronic or degenerative illness such as cancer. It is also valuable to know if he *fears* he may have a dread disease. One woman committed suicide out of the fear that she had a brain tumor, but when the autopsy was performed none was found; her thinking was so constricted that she felt she would rather commit suicide than die of her imagined brain tumor.

None of the above criteria, with the exception of a specific and lethal plan, should be considered highly dangerous alone. As the information is gathered, it should be considered as a whole to determine if a pattern is beginning to form. For example, in the situation of a depressive fifty-three-year-old divorced man who recently lost his job, who says that nobody cares anymore, and that he is going to drive his car off a bridge *tonight,* the counselor begins to see a fairly serious suicide pattern evolving which without intervention could easily result in a completed suicide.

4. *Develop a plan of action.* The individuals with the highest suicide lethality will need the most action on the part of the counselor. If the situation seems out of control, the minister should try to get the individual to a hospital, at least for forty-eight-hour observation. (It is valuable to know the laws of your state in this regard.) In other cases the individual may only need several sessions with the pastor to help him adapt to a recent loss or other stress; in this case the suicide lethality is quite low but his threatening suicide is a way of asking for help. In still other cases, the minister will feel he cannot counsel the person effectively and will transfer him to a specialist. His job is not done until the suicidal individual is in coun-

seling with the specialist, i.e., transferral is more than just "recommending a good psychiatrist." He must actually get the person an appointment, perhaps even drive him to the door.

In spite of attempts of ministers, mental health professionals and agencies, people still commit suicide. This has a very disruptive effect upon the close family and friends as well as the counselor or minister who was dealing with them. The next chapter will focus on what happens to the people a suicide victim leaves behind.

NOTES

1. Erich Lindemann, "Symptomatology and Management of Acute Grief," *Pastoral Psychology* XIV:36 (September, 1963): 8–18.

2. Paula Clayton, Lynn Desmarais, and George Winokur, "A Study of Normal Bereavement," *American Journal of Psychiatry* CXXV:2 (1968): 168–78.

3. P. Marris, *Widows and Their Families* (London: Routledge & Kegan Paul, 1958).

4. See Chapter 1, p. 3.

5. See Theodore J. Curphey's article in *The Cry for Help,* ed. Norman L. Farberow and Edwin S. Shneidman (New York: McGraw-Hill, 1965), pp. 118–28; Avery D. Weisman, "The Psychological Autopsy and the Potential Suicide," *Bulletin of Suicidology* (December, 1967): 15-24; Paul W. Pretzel et al., "Psychological Autopsy" (Paper read at SPC staff meeting, Los Angeles, March 21, 1969); and Avery D. Weisman and Robert Kastenbaum, *The Psychological Autopsy: A Study of the Terminal Phase of Life,* Community Mental Health Monographs (New York: Behavioral Publications Inc., 1968).

6. Norman L. Farberow and Maria D. Simon, "A Suicide Tale of Two Cities: An Intercultural Study" (Los Angeles: Suicide Prevention Center, mimeographed and unpublished n.d.), p. 19.

7. See Norman L. Farberow's article in *The Cry for Help,* pp. 298–303.

8. See especially Norman Tabachnick, "Interpersonal Relations in Suicidal Attempts," *Archives of General Psychiatry* III (January, 1961): 16–21; Michael L. Peck, "The Relation of Suicidal Behavior to Characteristics of the Significant Other" (Ph.D. thesis, The University of Portland, Portland, Oregon, 1965); and Michael L. Peck, "The Suicidal Family and the Double Bind" (Los Angeles: Suicide Prevention Center, January 26, 1966, mimeographed and unpublished).

9. Peck, "The Suicidal Family and the Double Bind," p. 2.

10. Ibid., pp. 3–4.

11. The reader can refer to the statistical results listed in Appendix B.

12. See especially Norman L. Farberow, "The Psychology of Suicide" (Los Angeles: Suicide Prevention Center, January 12, 1968, mimeographed and unpublished), p. 5; Norman L. Farberow, Samuel M. Heilig, and Robert E. Litman, *Techniques in Crisis Intervention: A Training Manual* (Los Angeles: Suicide Prevention Center, 1968), pp. 1–3.

13. See the definition in the Glossary and in the section on crisis in Chapter 5.

14. I am sometimes asked whether, in fact, a suicide should be prevented since man is a free agent. I suggest that the reader who is interested in this issue read Paul Pretzel's article, "Philosophical and Ethical Considerations of Suicide Prevention," *Bulletin of Suicidology,* Department of Health, Education and Welfare (July, 1968): 30–35. To briefly explain my own position: my clinical stance is to do everything within my power to aid a person in not committing suicide until he can convince me that doing so is a rational act. This stance is based on four observations about suicide: (1) The person who wants to commit suicide usually has ambivalent feelings about doing it. (2) The suicide crisis is usually of short duration. Individuals who have been prevented from killing themselves have later thanked friends and relatives who restrained them. (3) People who are considering suicide frequently have cognitive constriction, i.e., they have difficulty seeing the options available to them. For example, "Either I have to get my husband back or I will have to commit suicide." It is my job to help them discover other options. (4) Frequently the person who wants to commit suicide because "life is empty" is reacting to a recent loss which when worked through will allow him to fill the void and find meaning in life again.

If an individual is able to convince me that he does not have ambivalent feelings, is not suffering from depression, cognitive constriction, or a recent loss, and that his decision is totally rational, then I could conceive of letting him do what he wants. I have not encountered such a person and I doubt that I ever will. When an individual comes to me saying he wants to commit suicide, he is already betraying his ambivalence and is crying for help. Otherwise, why would he come?

15. Farberow, Heilig, and Litman, *Techniques in Crisis Intervention: A Training Manual.*

16. See Glossary for a definition of resources.

3. THE DYNAMICS OF THE SUICIDE GRIEF: EMOTIONAL REACTION

A Case of Grief in the Family (continued)

Let us return to the circumstances surrounding the suicide of Alice Dickinson.

Time does not stop to enable a recently bereaved person to gather his wits about him. He must plan for the funeral, the burial, and the many details that have to be handled right after the death. Bob Dickinson felt as if his head was swimming. In his own words, "I was an emotional mess for a few weeks."

At first, Bob just couldn't believe it was happening. The hospital was not able to keep her body for long so he had to locate a funeral director immediately. He didn't know where to go or what to do. His twenty-year-old daughter assisted him: "I think my daughter helped quite a bit . . . she was in a little bit better shape than I was, and she did most of the arranging . . . I went with her when we selected the casket and things like that. But as far as the other arrangements, she made them."

Already, with his wife dead only a few hours, Bob began to question why she had killed herself and what he had done to cause it. He began to think about the events that had preceded the death and how he might have prevented it. Later he reminisced, "She was eating then, but at night she wasn't sleeping real good, and she really was having a rough time. But we didn't know how rough it was . . . women go through that [menopause] and, you know, you just slough it off, I guess . . . she had been feeling bad for quite a while, and then I think it was Sunday we went back into the canyon, and it was kind of warm. We were sitting on a rock by a little stream, and she said it was the best she had felt for a long time. That was Sunday, and I think . . . [her death] was a Tuesday. I just really didn't pay as much attention to it as I should have." Already, guilt had begun to grip him; like a vulture it was sinking its claws into him and would not let him go in the weeks and months to come.

Bob was satisfied with the funeral and especially with his wife's priest, who officiated. "The only thing I objected to . . . is this viewing business. I just don't like it. . . . If you know them when they're alive, why not remember them that way?"

To this day Bob is not sure how his children feel about their mother's death—they never shared these feelings with each other. He did notice behavioral changes in his children. His eldest son was in college in New York City at the time. "My daughter called him, and he passed out. . . . Then when my son finally came home he came by airplane, and he was an absolute mess. His eyes were swollen shut. He had some kind of nervous reaction and it took three or four days to get over it . . . his face puffed up . . . the day of the funeral we sent him back to friends, and we figured he would be better there."

Bob is not certain how his eleven-year-old daughter felt. He said she cried a little but has never talked about her mother's suicide.

His other son was a junior in high school at the time. "He was pretty good [in school] when my wife died . . . it [the grief] probably did have a bearing. . . . His schoolwork suffered. . . . He is a very, very bright kid, and . . . he ended up with all F's." The boy left home soon afterwards. Bob is not certain where he is now, although he has reason to believe he is in Alaska.

Bob went back to work right after the funeral, and the subsequent weeks and months were very hard for him. A year and a half after the death he said, "Oh, I can talk about it a lot more than I could for six months there—I couldn't even think about it without breaking up. . . . I'm still not—you know, I'm a little upset." He was especially depressed in the first six months after the death: "Well, you know, when you think about lots of things, you contemplate joining her, you know. I guess everybody does that, right?" When I asked him how often he had contemplated committing suicide he said, "Oh, I guess there for a while at least once a week. Just kind of a depression that you get in, but it's pretty hard to shake it I'll tell you."

Bob said the depression began to lift after six to seven months, though it would still recur on occasion. "Oh, I'd say about after the first of this year [the depression lifted]. But around Christmas time

I got very depressed again because everything was brought back, around the holidays and all. I really wasn't over it yet, and then the holidays came on and I got depressed . . . I didn't sleep as well . . . I think I drank more, not hard alcohol, but I used to drink a lot of beer, because beer has a kind of tranquilizing effect. I think I drank more beer probably than I did in my life."

In response to a question about his feelings toward his own death he said, "Well, right now I'm not looking forward to it. Although a few months ago I would have welcomed it, I think. If I'd have dropped dead of a heart attack I probably would have been delighted. But now things are looking up and I'm certainly not looking forward to going."

For quite a while the depression affected Bob's sleep. "I was sleeping maybe four hours a night for months. I'd get up in the morning early and play the stereo and that went on for quite a while— six months anyhow. . . . I'm kind of getting back to normal. But it takes a while, as I say. . . . I guess it took my mind off things. And I used to play the stereo night and day for months. And after I straightened out I didn't feel like I needed to play it as much as I did." Bob felt this was a way to avoid the deep pangs of loneliness that were gripping him.

During his period of grieving, Bob has at times felt irritated at his wife. As he said, ". . . [suicide] does put an awful burden on the remaining." Much more on his mind, still, are those feelings of guilt which had begun to plague him within hours of Alice's death. "And I kept thinking, too, for her to be driven to that extreme, knowing how she loved the kids and everything, and I'm sure she loved me and all, and it just was inconceivable to me that she could have been that sick and me not know it."

I asked Bob if he felt he had been a little insensitive. "Yeah, I mean I lived with her twenty-one years—you kind of get to know somebody after that. And not to know that they were that far mentally—well, you have to be mentally unbalanced, really, to do it. I mean, naturally, I felt guilty for not being more compassionate or something. . . . I do know one thing, I will be more compassionate with my new wife, because I wouldn't ever want to think that I would have neglected her. Not that I did my other wife, but I think I would be . . . a better husband, really, to the second one, because of the first. . . . I think in a way I kind of took my wife for granted and it won't happen again."

When I asked Bob what helped him most in getting over the death of his wife, he suggested four things. First, he said, "I think one of the things is thinking about other people rather than yourself . . . because I did favors for other people around here, you know, in fact I still do, and I get enjoyment out of doing that. And really I think that's the kind of thing that helped me as much as anything."

Friends were a second source of help for Bob. Most of his old friends had dropped away after Alice's death. After about four months he decided to join a computer dating service to meet some women. Of this he says, "I found people that were in the same boat I was. I met some really nice people. . . . I used to go out a couple times a week. They were all women who had lost their husbands or were divorced or something—they all had problems, so at least you know someone else who is in the same boat." Bob had no relatives in the area. At his office, "There were a couple of the girls that were very understanding. And one of them I guess I got to really love her—she was that understanding. Of course . . . she was married, but she was the type that was really there when I needed somebody to lean on, talk to or something . . . she cared, and I knew she cared for me. . . . I think you tend to love more. I don't know how to ex-plain it, but I mean I thought a lot about a lot of people, and it seems as though you just wanted somebody to love, really. In a differ-ent way than you love your children. . . . As I say, it all seemed to center on this one girl in the office. She saw me through quite a rough period." The people at Bob's office did not attach any stigma to the manner of his wife's death. He sensed their caring for him.

A third help for Bob in his grief was an adult group at a local Presbyterian church. Before joining the group Bob had not attended church very much. One day about six or seven months after his wife's death he spotted an advertisement for the group in a local paper. Later Bob related, "I remember the first time I went down there and I just couldn't bring myself to go in . . . but finally I de-cided, I'm going to, so I finally went in and I'm glad I did. . . . It's really done [a lot] for me. . . ." In this group Bob acquired many new friends to replace the old ones who drifted away after his wife died.

One of these new friends became his fiancée. This was the fourth thing Bob felt had helped him with his grief. She has given him the opportunity to refocus the love he had invested in Alice toward someone else. About his fiancée Bob said, "Not only do you have to have love, but you also have to have somebody to boost your ego, I guess you might say, and when you're left alone you really don't have anyone to compliment you or anything like that. . . . And then when you find somebody you love and she loves you, that gives you that feeling . . . I think [feeling worthwhile is] almost as important as love, really."

After a year and a half, Bob Dickinson is still feeling the effects of Alice's suicide. He is looking forward to marrying again, but he carries with him the scars of a difficult but fairly typical suicide grief period. He still feels guilty about not doing enough for Alice, but he is trying to make this guilt work for him by being more caring in his new relationships. In many ways, with the help of his friends, with the support of his wife-to-be, and with the help of his church, he has adapted to the grief better than many people do after a suicide. Yet it has been, and will continue to be, a difficult time for him. The grief did not stop after a week or a month or a year. It is still with him and it will continue to be with him, even in his new marriage.

Seven Dynamics of Grief

The case of Bob Dickinson illustrates many of the dynamics of the suicide grief, which we are going to discuss in this and the next chapter. In the present chapter I will outline the seven basic dynamics which appear in *both* suicide and non-suicide grief reactions. I will describe how in each of these phases the suicide grief is similar to or different from the non-suicide grief. It should be noted immediately that the grief following suicide is not a totally different phenomenon. It is still a grief reaction. The minister's experience in helping members of his congregation to cope with death is valuable when he is faced with a suicide situation. Yet the suicide grief is distinct from the normal grief reaction, in the way and the extent to which each of these seven dynamics affects the survivor. What I am trying to say is that grief following any death, no matter what the cause, contains the basic elements of any other grief; yet how suicide survivors react varies from the typical reaction after a non-suicidal death.

The seven dynamics of grief are: (1) shock; (2) catharsis; (3) depression; (4) guilt; (5) preoccupation with the loss; (6) anger; and (7) reality.[1] In speaking of the dynamics or the phases of grief I do not wish to leave the reader with the impression that these are cut-and-dried, that the bereaved after finishing phase three will go immediately to phase four and so forth. It is not a linear progression; the seven dynamics of grief are listed in the order they generally appear. For example, although guilt may first be felt ten minutes after the death and continue for several years, the effect of shock is generally more dominant at that time. The seven dynamics are to be considered as seven major aspects of an individual's typical pattern of adaption to the traumatic loss involved in death.

1. Shock. In the first few hours, and off and on for the following two weeks after the death (and in some cases for short periods after that) the bereaved go into periods of shock. When death comes to a family, often the agony of the separation is so intense that the mind numbs the pain, as it does in any shock reaction, until later when the body can better accept it. The person is in a sense anesthetized against the overwhelming experience he is facing. Frequently individuals will say they "just can't believe it." They may act as if nothing has happened or behave in a wooden, mechanical way as they plan for the funeral.

During this period of his grief, Bob Dickinson felt helpless and numbed by the loss. In another case, the surviving spouse said of this period, "I felt nothing." Still another sat down and for several hours was unaware of anything going on around her. The wife of a fifty-year-old man who committed suicide described the first two weeks this way: "I was in shock, I guess. . . . Even when I went back to work I did my work, I did everything I was supposed to do, but it really seems like it was in a dream. I had to go to so many offices, Social Security and God knows what. If you ask me today where they were, I couldn't tell you."

A non-suicide spouse said, "When the doctor came in and told me he was dead, it was quite a shock. In fact they had to give me a couple of shots there in the hospital . . . and there were so many things that had to be done. I think I went through them *almost automatically* at the time, because they had to be done . . . and that's the way it was the first few days. After that the realization really started hitting me, and it started coming back." (Italics mine.) One man told me that after he heard the news he acted as if nothing much had happened. He went to the scene of his wife's death and made arrangements for the body to be removed. He said it was as if he were acting "automatically, like a robot."

The period of shock covers more than just the first few days; it can last longer and recur later for short periods of time. One woman, whose husband had hung himself, described how she felt at the funeral: "I think my feeling at the funeral was like I was watching a movie that I wasn't in, really. That's the way I felt—I felt like I wasn't really involved, I was just sort of sitting and watching it all go by, you know."

The reader should be aware—contrary to popular belief—that the shock period, in fact the whole grief process, is not noticeably different for non-suicide survivors who die suddenly (such as by heart attack, accident, etc.) than for the bereaved of those who were sick for long periods of time. Frequently after an individual has been dying and in pain for some time, the survivors will say they are "relieved" or "glad he didn't have to suffer anymore," but they will suffer the same shock and pain of grief as do survivors after a sudden death. It is important for the minister who is dealing with the bereaved not to assume that because they say they are "relieved" they are not suffering much. They are!

Both suicide and non-suicide spouses suffer much the same shock. Both are numbed by the loss and there is not much difference in the suicide and non-suicide grief at this point. It should be noted, though, as with Mr. Dickinson, that questions of "why" are beginning to be asked by the suicide survivors. This questioning becomes more important as the process of grief continues, but already at this early juncture in the grief process one can see differences between the suicide and non-suicide grief process.

2. Catharsis. The phase of shock is usually brief (though it may return from time to time later), and the release of emotion (catharsis) then begins. The stark reality of the loss begins to grip the bereaved. When one emotion is released, others are often forthcoming. In this stage the feelings of which I speak in later phases begin to emerge.

Some people have said they became hysterical during this period. Others do not express grief as dramatically but feel it just the same inside. Catharsis frequently dominates the first few days through the end of the first or second week. It is usually at a high point around the time of the funeral. In the case of Bob Dickinson, he found himself crying and fighting off tears for several weeks after the death. In fact, when talking about it a year and a half later, he had a difficult time to keep from crying. One husband whose wife had leaped to her death came out of his shock momentarily to find himself driving on the San Bernardino Freeway in Los Angeles. To quote him, "That's when it sort of *hit* me, and I pulled over and stopped and cried." During this period of catharsis the fact that a great loss has occurred begins to dawn upon the survivors. It is frequently felt as an overpowering emotion that cannot be controlled and usually it takes little counseling effort to aid a survivor in expressing it.

Crying is one of the most common ways of expressing grief. In our society crying is generally easier for women than for men. It should not be assumed that, because an individual has not openly cried, he is not "catharting." About one-fourth of bereaved spouses have indicated that they had "not cried to speak of since [their] spouse died," and yet most of them adapted well to their grief. What was striking was that suicide spouses tended to cry more than non-suicide spouses, and they tended to have more difficulty in their grief work. This is not to say that one shouldn't cry. Rather, I am taking issue with what seems to be a popular assumption among writers in the study of grief, that crying is almost *essential* to good grief work and that the absence of it is a bad sign. On the contrary, although crying and other ways of expressing the full weight of grief are important, I believe crying (at least very much crying) is not necessary for an adaptive grief reaction. What we need to do is to let the bereaved feel free to express their emotions in their own way.

Possibly because the bereaved feel uncomfortable with their emotions in public, they frequently want a good amount of time alone shortly after the death, and problems occur when company is forced upon them. Bob Dickinson appreciated having time alone: "At that particular time [the first three or four weeks] it was better that way, really, so I could get a hold of myself." One widow put it this way: "I didn't want anybody—it's like a wounded animal, you want to go away and lick your wounds and heal. You want to lie down and bleed to death, but do it by yourself, and when you're ready to get up, you get up. . . . They kept saying, you have to have people with you. I said no. I've got to face these ghosts. I've got to live in this house. Let me work it out. . . ."

A man in his middle forties described his feelings about wanting to be alone after his wife died of cancer: "There are times when you want to be left alone, times when you just want to sit and think, whether it's thinking or just staring off into space with no thoughts in your mind. You don't like to have somebody come in and interrupt those thoughts. A lot of times I found that when I wanted to talk to someone I'd go over and visit, all of a sudden I'd get restless and want to take off, and I would excuse myself, I had something to do. But when somebody's in your home it's pretty hard . . . everybody's well meaning, but you can't say I'm tired of talking, get out. . . . Most of the conversation, as I think back, with the men was basketball, baseball, sports, what have you. It was more on a current day-to-day basis, with no references to the past unless I brought it up, and then they would talk with me. . . . I would much rather have it that way, in other words *for me to set my own pace* as to what I would like to talk about, because they can't tell how I feel at any particular time." (Italics mine.)

Generally, what the bereaved desire at this early period of time is the opportunity to talk to people on their own terms. In other words, if they feel like it they can seek out the opportunity to talk with someone, and if they want to be alone and "face these ghosts" they can do that. What is *not* helpful in my opinion is for the survivors to go to either extreme for very long periods—to talk to no one, or never to be alone to face their feelings. The minister needs to watch for either of these extremes—they can be warning flags of future problems.

How do the suicide survivors fare during this period? Besides the overwhelming weight of grief, the suicide survivor must deal with the fact that it was a suicide death, and all that this entails. Several decisions are made as the survivors move out of the period of shock and begin the catharsis phase. For one, they decide whether or not to tell others it was a suicidal death, and whom they will tell. The suicide survivors also begin to feel the stigma of the suicidal death.

Many emotions run through the minds of the bereaved. Frequently they feel very ashamed and sense the censure of neighbors and friends much more than really exists. As a result they may move, or in other ways break many of the ties with friends that could help them through their period of grief.

A forty-five-year-old widow originally from France described her feelings about her husband's suicide this way: "I've never talked to anybody about this. At first I felt very uncomfortable in the office, because I didn't know whether they knew or not. . . . As far as I know there are about three or four people in the company that know. But sometimes I have a feeling that everybody knows, because nobody ever asks a question. They just say he had an accident. . . . Except one man, he made a remark, and he was quickly shut up by someone else. . . . So now I just sometimes wonder, do they know or don't they know."

In summary, the added element of suicide begins to affect the grief reaction even more during catharsis than it did during the shock period, but still not as much as in some of the phases which will follow. During these first few weeks after the death the important decisions of whether or not to tell people it was a suicide, and who will be told, have to be made. These early decisions will dramatically affect the course of the total grief reaction as it continues to unfold.

3. Depression. After the funeral is over and acquaintances have stopped talking about the deceased and go on with their business as usual, the survivors have bouts with depression. These periods of depression seem to come and go with diminishing frequency and duration. Some anxiety and angry outbursts associated with the depression also occur Often these periods of despair and depression can be incubation periods for later expressions of guilty and angry feelings concerning the deceased. Because of the unusual aspects of the grief reaction—exaggerated guilt feelings and long periods of depression and anger at the dead person—the bereaved may consider suicide during these periods of despair.

Most people indicate that after about six months the bouts with depression lessen and they feel more able to manage them. Mr. Dickinson said it was after about the sixth month that his depression lifted, though he said at sentimental times of the year (Christmas, anniversaries, anniversary of the death), he felt "low" again. One widow put it this way: "For about five months after the death of my husband, I was very depressed and unhappy. I took hold of myself. One, I have five children and they needed me. Two, I had to start communicating with adults, so I started to go out. This helped tremendously."

Each person experiences depression in a different way. Here is one man's description: "Sometimes it would just last for half an hour, an hour or so. I would go into the bedroom or the den where I was by myself. . . . A lot of things were going through my mind, but there were more blanks than anything else. It was just a kind of . . . not thinking of anything so that you can get a fresh start, and the gears mesh again. . . . In other words, millions of thoughts ran through my mind but not anything specific . . . so many of them that they were just like a brass band, and yet other times it would be completely blank, where I would just sit and stare at the wall and there were no thoughts coming through. . . . One of the things I'd made up my mind to was that I wasn't going to dwell on the bad things that had happened during our marriage; I was going to look on the bright side of our marriage, and yet after a couple, three months I realized that that wasn't good either, that I had to look at it as it was, the good and the bad things. At first I think I tried to concentrate on the good things, but sometimes I think it made it even worse."

During the period of shock certain psychosomatic changes occur as a result of the emotional distress, such as tightness in the throat, a feeling of lack of muscle coordination and power, shortness of breath, abdominal distress, etc. Throughout the grief process there can be dramatic physical disturbances. During the time when depression is dominant, there appears to be more physical distress, "nervousness," and the like. The bereaved need to be aware that grief is an emotion, and like all emotions it can involve physical changes. Lindemann and others have done research on this and have found psychosomatic reactions to grief to include rheumatoid arthritis, asthma, and spastic colitis.[2] These can especially be a problem if an individual is "stuck" in his grief. Westberg states, "Some of these people who have physical symptoms of distress have stopped at one of the stages. . . . Unless someone can help them to work through the emotional problems involved in the stage in which they seem to be fixed, they will remain ill."[3]

A widow in her forties described her fatigue, "nervousness," and psychomatic problems a year after her husband shot himself: "I am very nervous. And for that reason just a month ago I went to the doctor . . . maybe it's just loneliness, I don't know. And I find myself yelling at my son sometimes at night. . . . And I don't want to do that because it's not his fault. But sometimes I just can't help it. So he gave me a tranquilizer. . . . And I had other side effects, and I think it was just plain nerves. I used to break out at night. I'd sit here and watch TV, and I'd start itching all over. And my eyes played tricks on me, I kept seeing black spots . . . which is just plain nerves, because now when I feel real nervous I take a tranquilizer and it has stopped. He did say . . . it's just emotional . . . and even though it's quite some time ago, it still—a person still reacts to it [the death]. Maybe I'm just late in reacting. I don't know."

Speaking of fatigue, the same woman said, "And yet, I have a sneaking suspicion that tiredness is sort of escape . . . of being lonesome. So I go to sleep—I don't have to think about it . . . I don't have much to look forward to at night, so I'm tried and go to sleep."

Suicide survivors are plagued with physical ailments much more than the non-suicide survivors. They also tend to feel more fatigued. In response to the question, "I have not been as healthy since the death of my spouse (i.e. asthma, rheumatism, colds, rashes, headaches, etc.)," 54% of the suicide survivors, over against only 13% of the non-suicide survivors, believed that they had been sick more.[4] This may indicate that the suicide survivors are "swallowing" their grief more and experiencing it in physical symptoms. By holding in their grief the suicide survivors are much more prone to have all forms of physical ailments than the non-suicide bereaved. This is a crucial difference between the suicide and non-suicide grief reaction.

Besides the psychosomatic occurrences, as mentioned above, the survivors may experience suicide feelings, ideas, or may even attempt suicide—"to join him"—during the period of depression. Frequently, the greatest severity of the suicide risk is during the first six months of grief, and especially about three months after the death. Ideas of suicide and suicide attempts occur more frequently among the survivors of a suicide than of a non-suicide death. Dorpat and others have noticed this tendency and have described a fairly high amount of suicide ideation and activity among survivors of a suicide.[5]

One widow related, "I felt like killing myself when my mother died. Only the love and support of my husband saw me through that unhappy time. I believe if it were not for my children I would have taken my own life when my husband died. I had a very strong urge to join him."

Many close survivors of a death, whether or not it is a suicide, think somewhat about suicide in their moments of despair. To non-suicide survivors it seems that suicide is a less viable option than it is to suicide survivors, for whom the idea of suicide as "a way out" is always present. They have had close contact with it as a way of death, and even though they may detest it they still frequently toy with the idea in their moments of depression.

In the present research, 12% of the non-suicide survivors said they had thought about committing suicide. In contrast, 32% of the suicide survivors had ideas of suicide (one of them having actually attempted it.) Unfortunately, 20% of the subjects did not respond to the question at all, thus reducing the validity of this point in the research. However, the results do agree with other research in the field.

One of the five patterns found in the aftermath of a suicide in marital partners by Cain and Fast is a heightening of openly self-destructive impulses and behavior. In a sample of forty-five families who had come in for counseling after a suicide death, three had committed suicide and four more had attempted it. "For some, suicidal fantasies seemed alien or related only to their despondency as in a normal non-suicide grief reaction; but others experienced them quite consciously as self-punitive, identificatory, or even in a distorted way vengefully retaliatory."[6] Thus, besides the possibility of suicide ideation one would normally go through during grief, there are also the added fantasies within the survivors that relate directly to their spouses' suicide.

Morbid suicide preoccupation is also found in adults who as children lost parents by suicide. Dorpat states: "All the patients (17) had been more or less preoccupied with suicide since the time of their parent's suicide. . . . Several patients came to treatment with the chief complaint of a morbid and persistent fear of committing suicide. They felt doomed to kill themselves as their parents had."[7]

In summary, both suicide and non-suicide survivors experience periods of depression in the months following the funeral. For most people the cloud of depression begins to lift after the sixth month. One way this depression manifests itself is in physical symptoms— nervousness, headaches, fatigue, psychosomatic illnesses such as colitis, etc. Suicide survivors experience a great deal more physical ailments and disease than non-suicide survivors. This is another dramatic distinguishing mark of the difference between suicide and non-suicide grief. In their depression, the bereaved may also exhibit thoughts of suicide, or actively attempt it. The higher frequency of suicide ideation and activity among suicide survivors is still another distinguishing mark of the suicide grief reaction. In general, the special problems that suicide brings for the surviving spouse makes the already difficult period of depression even more troublesome.

4. Guilt. Feeling guilty is almost inevitable after any death of a loved one. In the case of Bob Dickinson, he began to ask himself *why* Alice had committed suicide, and how he might have caused it, only hours after her death. For a time afterwards he was contemplating suicide himself at least once a week. When it comes to differentiating the typical suicide and non-suicide grief, guilt is the major division. Both suicide and non-suicide survivors feel guilty, but the suicide survivors generally suffer from a greater, more pervasive guilt and their guilt does not diminish much with time. In other words, suicide works!

Let me explain what I mean by saying "suicide works." The statistical tests which discovered a greater amount of guilt among suicide survivors indicate that it does indeed work. That is, the individual who commits suicide is often angry and disappointed and uses suicide as a way to hurt the people around him. It is an angry, desperate gesture. Sometimes it is a type of mental blackmail in which the unconscious desire is to punish a disappointing individual[8] or, as Karon phrases it, an attempt to hurt someone else through the fantasy that killing oneself is effective retaliation.[9] The suicidal death is successful in making the surviving spouse feel guilty.

One widow described her feelings of guilt this way: "I really tried to torture myself. . . . He just said in the suicide note that I didn't love him the way he wanted me to love him. He was exchanging his life for a better life for me and the children, and he hoped that my next husband would love me as he did." Soon after the death, she said, "I was getting more and more hysterical—what did I do, you know—it was always what did I do to make him do this? Where did

I—I drove him to it—I did this—I did that." A year and a half after the death this woman said she still feels guilt about the death but figures he committed suicide because he was mentally sick (which is frequently a rationalization used by survivors in an attempt to eliminate some of the guilt they feel; it is only partly effective and frequently only veils the guilt which still exists).

The same woman now thinks, "Don't you suppose everybody who commits suicide does it to punish somebody? They don't do it to get rid of their self." She now has some insight into some of the underlying reasons for her husband's death. Thus she professes not to feel much of the original guilt she felt. But now she has a new type of guilt in which she feels as if she ought to feel guilty—"Now I feel guilty that I don't feel guilty," she says, "I am a hardhearted character." Like the claim of mental illness as the reason for the death, so this "feeling guilty for not feeling guilty" is another phase of the guilt which is particularly associated with a suicidal death. The amount of guilt felt is not really diminishing much with time, just changing its form of expression.

Four questions dealt directly with the survivor's guilt.[10] One tested whether the survivor felt he or she had somehow caused the death: "Although I don't like to think of it, I feel at times as if I were part of the cause of my spouse's death." The answers showed a dramatic difference between suicide and non-suicide survivors. Only a handful of non-suicide survivors felt this way, while over half of all suicide survivors felt guilty about being part of the cause of their spouses' death.

Another question was: "I often think I should have done more for my spouse before he/she died." The answers were again dramatic. Only 35% of the non-suicide survivors agreed, but 65% of the suicide survivors believed they could have done more for their deceased spouses. They entertained the somewhat grandiose assumption that they really could have controlled another's decision to take his own life.

A third question dealt with how the survivors had acted toward the deceased before death: "I feel guilty about some things I said and did before my spouse died." Of the suicide spouses, 69% agreed with this statement, compared to only 32% of the non-suicide spouses. I believe this question is a good test of the general guilt felt by the survivors in relation to the deceased. Most individuals, being human, may have said and done things that were "stupid," angry, or in haste in the weeks before a death, but those who feel "at peace" about the relationship do not feel much guilt. The individual who feels guilty dramatizes and dwells on these "bad" events and angry words. He relives these scenes and wishes he had acted differently. Mr. Dickinson, for example, remembers that he did not pay enough attention to his wife those last weeks and months. He still can recall, a year and a half later, scenes where Alice told him how bad she was feeling, and how he ignored them thinking they were only the result of menopause. Even today he would like to live those moments over again, though he realizes he cannot.

The final question on guilt was designed to test whether or not spouses felt guilty and ashamed about the *type* of death: "Although I feel I maybe shouldn't, at times I feel ashamed about the way my husband/wife died." The results again indicated guilt. Of the suicide spouses, 44% did feel ashamed and guilty that the manner of death was suicide.

It was mentioned before that the survivors after a suicide usually develop ways to explain why the deceased killed himself. Two of their most common reasons are "he was mentally ill" or "he was an alcoholic." Recently, with the rising suicide rate among young people in some parts of the country (like Los Angeles), "he was using drugs and accidentally overdosed" is the reason frequently given by parents. Another approach has been to blame someone else, such as his parents, his psychiatrist, or counselor, his boss who made him work so hard, etc. All are rationalizations to allay the guilt that the survivor feels. These seem to superficially help some of the survivors (especially "he was mentally ill") but they frequently only hide the individual's real guilt feelings. In other words, they do not help very much in alleviating the guilt feelings. There are other reactions to the guilt feelings such as overcompensating for the guilt by either portraying the deceased as perfect, or working hard for the betterment of mankind—especially for man's better emotional health—etc.

Related to the fourth dynamic of grief—guilt—is the fact that suicide survivors feel a certain stigma attached to the type of death, and they feel blamed by others for the death. They were asked to respond to the statements, "At times I have felt like I was being compelled to move residence because of what some people thought about my spouse dying," and "I have felt blamed by others to some extent for my spouse's death." In both cases the suicide spouses sensed more stigma and blame from others than did the non-suicide survivors. The reaction of the majority of suicide spouses whom I have encountered has been *not* to be very honest with friends and associates about the death. Instead of openly dealing with the fact that one's spouse has died by suicide, most of the feelings about the suicide are held within. This compounds the problems of grief and can also cause the spouse to perceive more stigma than might really exist.

Although there is some actual blaming by friends, neighbors, and business associates, it appears that a good part of the stigma is simply projection. It has been my experience that, in general, the survivors who are more open feel less stigma and blame.

Guilt has been dealt with as a negative emotion, but it can also be a positive one. One woman in her thirties put it this way: "It makes you a better person, because you stop and think twice before you scream at someone . . . because you think twice before saying something, because words can never be taken back, and I think now before I say something terribly unkind in anger. . . . Guilt is marvelous, because you can reverse it and make it work for you."

In summary, guilt highlights the major differences between the suicide and non-suicide grief reactions. The suicide survivor typically suffers under more guilt than the non-suicide survivor, and his guilt, though it may change its character, continues for months and years afterwards without decreasing very much in intensity. Guilt is still felt deeply by many suicide survivors a year or two after a death. For non-suicide survivors this is generally not the case.

Along with the guilt (and I believe related to it) is the stigma about the type of death that a suicide entails, and the perceived blame from others for the death. Non-suicide survivors do not experience these. This, plus the difficulties already inherent in a grief reaction, give the suicide survivors extra grief work to go through.

5. Preoccupation with the loss. Lindemann points out that there is often an intense preoccupation with the image of the deceased. An armed forces pilot reacted to the death of a close friend by constantly fantasizing him. He was an imaginary companion who ate, drank, and did everything with him. This experience is a form of unadaptive grief reaction and calls for therapeutic help. Most individuals do not focus on the deceased to such an extent.

Most close survivors experience a preoccupation with the loss. It is not a continuous thing, but it ebbs and flows. At times they seem to function normally; at other times they are so preoccupied with the loss that they are not able to accomplish anything. They are caught up in a fantasy world about the deceased. At this stage the bereaved may try to get back in the "groove," like it was before the loss, but he finds he is unable to do so.

> There is a restlessness, inability to sit still, moving about in an aimless fashion, continually searching for something to do. There is, however, at the same time, a painful lack of capacity to initiate and maintain organized patterns of activity. . . . The bereaved is surprised to find how large a part of his customary activity was done in some meaningful relation to the deceased and has now lost its significance.[11]

What is sad is that the person still feels the loss, but after the first few weeks, when he begins to move back into life again, no one talks much about his loss anymore. The outside world is still very much an alien environment to him, yet there is a kind of "conspiracy of silence" among his associates concerning the death.[12]

The preoccupation with the loss expresses itself in different ways. Bob Dickinson felt it somewhat, though not as much as other spouses do. He frequently felt this way during his periods of loneliness or in his guilt-laden ruminations over what he could have done differently so his wife would not have committed suicide. He tried to fight off or avoid being too preoccupied with his loss. He listened to his stereo for long hours to avoid loneliness and thinking about her death.

Preoccupation with loss can exhibit itself also in the apathy of the bereaved towards life and others, and unwillingness to give up an attachment to the bereaved (e.g., the armed forces pilot). Another way is for the bereaved to unconsciously act like the deceased—to the point of contracting the disease which the bereaved had before death. Most close family survivors will at times "experience" the deceased's presence with them, dream of him, smell his body odors or his pipe tobacco, hear his footsteps, or hear him calling them. This experience is a normal part of the grief reaction and becomes a problem only when the bereaved become so preoccupied with these things that they are unable to function in other areas of life. When this preoccupation becomes an obsession, it becomes unadaptive. It is when a preoccupation with the loss and the deceased involves so much of the bereaved's life that he does not function in the normal activities of life, that it becomes serious.

The following are examples of ways in which survivors have experienced a preoccupation with their loss. A forty-three-year-old salesman, after more than a year, still lived in a ritualized way: "I've stayed in the same house, and kept things in the same order. . . . Because that's the way they were, and that's the way she put them, and I'm still form-living, so to speak, to that extent . . . this girl here lived with me for a while, and in a way I'm glad that I could pull it off, that I could have another woman there and feel content with her there; on the other hand, I feel very guilty about doing it to her, her being there, because she didn't touch anything —her presence is not there. In my physical surroundings she was afraid to touch anything, or move anything, or do anything like that. . . . I don't think I have her [his deceased wife] on a pedestal, but I do have her on a very high rung."

Another survivor said she idealized her husband for quite a while. She would sit and daydream about him and all his good attributes. A year after his death she described the experience this way: "I found that the more I idealized him the more unhappy I became and the more I felt the sense of loss. On the other hand, when I tried to think of the bad things, and say, 'Jeez, you're better off,' I felt guilty, and that was just as bad as the other way."

Another spouse would pretend sometimes that her husband was not dead but just away on a trip. She put it this way: "I sometimes find comfort going to the cemetery and spending time in prayer feeling very close to my husband. There are times I try to think of him just being away on a trip. I also feel like a person all alone." For her, to escape into the fantasy that her husband is still alive and will be coming home fills a little of the void of her deep loneliness.

Still another wife said that she frequently felt her deceased husband's presence with her, dreamed about him, etc. "I wish I'd stop dreaming such weird dreams of him, always as though he were still alive or saving me from fire or to come go live in his world. I always feel his presence in the room when I do this type dream. Feel it too strong. Smell his body odor, etc." What is interesting in her description of her dreams is that again the spouse is alive. Her dreams do not describe—unless she didn't tell me—the way he committed suicide. These dreams may also express that she is toying with the idea of committing suicide—"come go live in his world."

A final example is of a very unadaptive response. This fifty-year-old Czechoslovakian man still visited his wife's grave every day. He had already remarried and divorced. (His new wife did not want to go to the grave with him every day.) His gross preoccupation with his deceased wife, to the exclusion of his new wife, left him divorced, bitter and lonely, waiting to die. He had focused himself so much on his deceased spouse that he was not functioning well in reality any more. Every night he prayed that he would die. This was quite a change from the vibrant person he had been before the death.

How do suicide survivors fare during this phase of grief? There is no real significant difference between the suicide and non-suicide survivors regarding the dynamic of preoccupation with the loss. Although the dynamics of guilt sometimes become entwined with this phase, the preoccupation with the loss is not one of the factors that distinguish the suicide and non-suicide survivors.

6. Anger. This dynamic of grief is usually a good sign because it frequently means the person is beginning to come out of his depression and his constant focusing on the dead person, and is expressing himself openly again. He complains about those who have been around him in the final stages of death and during his previous phases of grief (which include doctors, nurses, ministers, etc.). Mr. Dickinson said he never felt very angry after the death of his wife, though he said he was a little more irritable from time to time. On several occasions he caught himself "snapping" at his children which he later felt badly about.

The greater amount of irritability which Mr. Dickinson felt at times is experienced by many of those who are bereaved. Of the total group studied, 38% (both suicide and non-suicide) agreed that "Since my spouse died I get annoyed or irritated more easily than I used to." There was no significant difference between suicide and non-suicide survivors here. Thus this irritation or generalized hostility is not a factor that distinguishes the suicide survivors from the non-suicide survivors.

People grieving the death of someone close focus their anger on different people and objects, such as doctors or nurses who attended the deceased, the ambulance driver, the police who were too slow in reaching the scene of an accident or suicide, etc. Friends and relatives who are close to the person either before or after the death frequently have some anger leveled at them also.

The minister, rabbi, or priest who is with the bereaved after the death will on occasion receive this anger. I believe the anger at ministers can frequently be seen as veiled anger at God. The minister is, in the eyes of the survivor, the representative of God. Questions such as "Why did God do this to me?" "How could God let him do something like that?" and many others are asked implicitly or explicitly of the minister.

One man, a self-styled atheist whose wife had committed suicide, said he was furious with God. He said he could not understand this because he had not thought about religion or gone to church for over fifteen years. Another spouse whose husband "accidentally" shot himself through the head said, "Why did [God] do this? Why did he take him? Of course at this time you only think about your own grief. You don't think about the millions of other people who have gone through this. But all I could think about was my own situation, how I felt, and how I thought God was very unjust, that he would have taken this man away from his home and his family."

A woman in her middle thirties whose husband died of a heart attack expressed anger at her husband for leaving her with the mess of a small business which he had recently opened and which went bankrupt six months after his death. She said, "I've said many times that if he's able to run by the time I get up there, and he is breathing . . . by God he'd better start running, because I'm coming after him with every lousy, stinking unpaid bill. Every little business nuance he forgot to tell me about. There was a desk full of stuff that he should have taken care of, that any human being should, instead of dumping the whole thing in my lap. And man, I'm not irritated, I'm furious. And when I get there, by God, he'd better take off. And I'm not kidding, because that was a miserable trick to do . . . . But I think it's a kind of miserable trick to drop dead."

Another spouse whose husband shot himself maintained she did not feel much anger but said she dreamed about her husband asking her not to be angry with him anymore. "I dreamt about him. And he talked to me—not very much, just apologizing, not to be angry with him, but he was peaceful now, and he has never been in his whole life. I actually saw him saying it."

One final illustration of anger is a woman garment worker who said her anger at her husband was what helped her through the first few weeks and months. She started feeling very guilty, asking herself why she had "caused" him to kill himself, but a close friend told her that her husband was "no good or he wouldn't have committed suicide"—that he didn't love her, etc. "And he got me so angry that I really think anger's what held my sanity together for the next few days. . . . I was brought up pretty religious, and I felt like I was practically blaspheming the dead to even think the thoughts he was trying to make me think. . . . If I'd have kept feeling as guilty as I did when it first happened, I wouldn't have been any good to my children. It was all in thought. I don't think I said a word out loud against him to anybody, but I was sure thinking it. I mean it's a terrible thing to say, but I think at the moment I could have gotten up and hung him over, and the kids and his kids."

These illustrations indicate that the anger which the bereaved feel can be focused on anything or anybody. Many close survivors, especially spouses, feel angry at the deceased. This anger is usually not verbalized; survivors usually feel guilty for having such feelings and therefore try to ignore them, pretending they do not have them. Anger at the deceased is especially important when it occurs in the suicide survivors. Although suicide survivors do not seem to have a greater amount of generalized anger and hostility, they have significantly more anger at the deceased. While 22% of the non-suicide spouses said they had felt anger at their deceased spouses, over half (54%) of all suicide spouses had felt anger at their deceased partners. Thus greater anger at the deceased is another distinguishing mark of the suicide grief. It is something that is not usually talked about but which is felt deeply.

7. Adapting to reality. This final phase of the grief process stems from an awareness of the futility of continued withdrawal from reality. The person is really a changed or new person, because he has gone through the loss of a loved one and now lives on, facing life hopefully a stronger, deeper person, better able to help others go through the same experience. Each crisis such as grief is both a "danger and an opportunity." The individual's reaction to the grief depends a lot on how others relate to him. He can either become an emotionally healthier person, or someone who never really accepts the death.

This last phase begins when the survivors have worked through much (though not all) of their feelings about the death and have chosen consciously or unconsciously to reconstruct a new life without the deceased. It occurs only after the survivors have seen how much of their life was tied up with the deceased and have started to fill the void in other ways—with other people, activities, and so forth.

The commitment to live a full life without the deceased is actually made over and over again. As one survivor put it, "It is an openness to live each day as it comes." In unadaptive grief reactions the survivor is still trying so hard to hold on to the deceased that he will not face up to reality.

Reaching the seventh phase of the grief process doesn't mean the bereaved will no longer experience any of the emotional dynamics of the previous six phases. The individual, though he will struggle with these feelings intermittently for years, has adapted fairly well to the loss and has opened himself up to the new possibilities in the present and future.

In the research done for this book it was found that in comparing those whose spouses had died from one to one and one-half years ago with those whose spouses died from one and one-half to two years ago, there was a significant difference in the working through of the various aspects of the grief reaction (except guilt). In other words, the grief reaction is not nearly finished after a year, as some counselors have believed, but is a continual process with significant growth occurring in the second year after the death. The survivors live with scars from the grief for many years, but as early as two or three weeks after the death they can begin the process of affirming reality and life without the deceased.

The only difference between the suicide and non-suicide grief in this final phase is that the suicide grief generally seems more sluggish and doesn't resolve as rapidly as the non-suicide grief. Outside of this, both suicide and non-suicide survivors have scars to live with but both can work through their grief in a satisfactory way.

Summary

These are the seven phases of the grief reaction. They are not a linear progression of stages; rather, they describe the seven major emotional dynamics which the bereaved experience, listed in the order they generally appear.

The major differences between the suicide and non-suicide grief are as follows. During the phase of catharsis, the feelings concerning the type of death (suicide) have to be expressed. At an early point after the death the stigma of suicide and blame from others are perceived, and the suicide spouse has to decide at this time if he will tell others that it was a suicide and whom he will tell. This is a difficult decision.

During the period of depression, especially around the third month, there seems to be more suicide ideation—more self-destructive impulses and behavior—among suicide survivors. There is also more illness and considerable fatigue with suicide survivors. This would indicate to this author that suicide survivors hold the grief within themselves more and act it out psychosomatically.

Probably the major difference between the suicide and non-suicide survivors is the greater amount of guilt associated with the suicide death. Connected with this guilt is a greater amount of anger at the deceased felt by suicide survivors. On the whole, the bereaved after a suicide have a more difficult task to accomplish in their grief work. This occurs mainly because of the added burden suicide places on those who grieve.

NOTES

1. I am indebted to the work of several other authors in the field of grief who have influenced my thinking in the development and testing of these seven dynamics of grief. These authors are Granger Westberg in his book *Good Grief* (Philadelphia: Fortress Press, 1962); Edgar Jackson's *Understanding Grief* (New York: Abingdon Press, 1957); Paul Irion in his books, and Erich Lindemann in his classic article, "Symptomatology and Management of Acute Grief" (*Pastoral Psychology* XIV:36 [September, 1963]: 8–18).

2. See Erich Lindemann, "Modifications in the Course of Ulcerative Colitis in Relationship to Changes in Life Situations and Reaction Patterns," *Journal of Nervous and Mental Disease* XXIX (1950): 706; and Lindemann, "Symptomatology and Management of Acute Grief," p. 13.

3. Westberg, *Good Grief*, p. 28.

4. See Appendix B for statistical results.

5. See the articles in the bibliography under the heading, "Suicide Grief." See especially all of the articles by Cain and Fast.

6. Albert C. Cain and Irene Fast, "The Legacy of Suicide: Observations on the Pathogenic Impact of Suicide Upon Marital Partners," *Psychiatry* XXIX:4 (1966): 410.

7. Theodore L. Dorpat, "Psychological Effects of Parental Suicide on Surviving Children" (Unpublished paper).

8. This concept is dealt with by Joost Meerlo in *Suicide and Mass Suicide* (New York: Grune & Stratton, 1962).

9. B. P. Karon, "Suicidal Tendency as the Wish to Hurt Someone Else and Resulting Treatment Techniques," *Journal of Individual Psychology* XX:2 (1964): 206–12.

10. The four questions were factor-analyzed and fall within one of the five factors—factor 2, guilt. Further explication of this guilt factor is made in the author's dissertation (see p. 113, n. 2). The statistical results of the guilt questions are included below in Appendix B.

11. Lindemann, "Symptomatology and Management of Acute Grief," p. 10.

12. Westberg, *Good Grief,* p. 48.

4. *THE DYNAMICS OF THE SUICIDE GRIEF:* *INTERPERSONAL AND DEMOGRAPHIC*

There are other factors of the suicide grief reaction which were not covered in Chapter 3—the individual's religious involvement, remarriage, the survivor's age and sex, and so forth. They are not always crucial to the grief reaction, but these different factors give the minister or counselor useful data on the total setting of a suicide situation. If, for example, you were Mr. Dickinson's minister or counselor, it would be important to find out what resource agencies or persons ("significant others") he is drawing upon for help in his grief. It would help you to know that at a church group he has met another woman whom he is planning to marry soon. You would also want to discover how his children have reacted to the death, how they are getting along at school and at home, etc. These important inputs could help you form a more complete picture of Mr. Dickinson's grief response. In the paragraphs that follow, various additional factors of the total grief response will be discussed.

Age, Sex, and Education

It can be seen from the survey findings listed in Appendix B that people in various stages of their middle years react much the same in their grief. This was true for both suicide and non-suicide survivors. Adolescents, on the other hand, physically "act out" their grief more than adults, as Jackson and others have indicated.[1] They may become juvenile delinquents. Children also act out their grief behaviorally more than adults. To quote Jackson, "The grief expressions of children are not likely to be shown in the same manner as those of mature years. The child's grief is more likely to be shown in physical symptoms. . . ."[2] Cain and Fast, in studying children aged four to fourteen who came for therapy after a parent's suicide, indicate that one of the dominant problems experienced by children is *guilt*. This will be explored more fully later in this chapter.[3]

In a study of people over age sixty-five who died by non-suicide means, Jackson found a lack of guilt feelings among the survivors but more psychosomatic illness resulting from the grief.[4] No valid information is available on how the aged react to a suicide. My guess (and I believe a sound one) is that their reaction would be much the same as that outlined in Chapter 3, with the exception that the aged would not experience as much guilt as middle-aged individuals. Finally, as Jackson has shown, there is more psychosomatic illness among the aged than among the rest of the population.

In the research for this book there appeared to be no significant differences between the grief reactions of men and women. Behaviorally they may "act out" their grief differently in some respects, women crying more freely and frequently than men, and men being more openly aggressive with their anger; yet the sex of the individual makes little difference as far as the basic grief process is concerned.

Interestingly, when non-suicide survivors who had a college education were compared with those who had at most a high school education, the college-educated were found to do a better job of accepting the loss. It may be that highly educated people have more resources to fall back on in times of crisis: they are better able to manipulate symbols within the intellectual sphere; they are more aware of counseling opportunities; they are aware of more individuals to whom they can talk about their grief. However, to college-educated people who lose a spouse by *suicide,* the shock seems just as devastating as among the less educated. The extra help that a college education seems to give the non-suicide survivors is no longer present, and their grief reaction is no different from that of non-college-educated individuals.

Religion and the Church

In the religious aspects of their grief responses, there seem to be no significant differences between suicide and non-suicide survivors.[5] There is a tendency, though not statistically significant, for suicide survivors to feel they have been more religious since the death (in contrast to non-suicide survivors). However, they felt that the church was *not* as helpful to them in their grief; this may be a reflection of the organized church's moral stance against suicide, or of the survivor's feeling that he would not be accepted within the church because of the suicide. Although there are exceptions, there does not appear to be any significant change of religious practices among either suicide or non-suicide survivors. Some individuals feel closer to God after the death and attend church more frequently. Others are angry at God and will not darken the door of a church. Still others, who had gone to church in the past only because their husbands or wives had, now no longer attend.

The lack of difference between the grief processes of church attenders and those who do not attend church is quite interesting. It indicates that regular church attenders generally have no better acceptance of the death; nor do they feel less guilt. One might wonder why the churches are not meeting the needs of these individuals any more than they are. It must be noted, however, that at the very worst, it appears the church does not harm the individual in his grief. To this observer the results indicate that churches need to come to terms more conclusively with death, life after death, and grief. These are central issues in religion and if they are neglected or inadequately handled the church is failing its people and its mission.

A comparison of Protestants and Roman Catholics led to an interesting finding. The Roman Catholic suicide survivor generally feels significantly more guilt than either Roman Catholic non-suicide survivors or all Protestant survivors (either suicide or non-suicide). This finding may suggest that the Roman Catholic Church's strong moral stand against suicide is contributing to a greater amount of guilt felt among Catholic suicide survivors. Catholic theologians may wish to consider the implications of their present position on suicide as it affects the survivors.

It was mentioned in the previous chapter that fairly soon after the death some survivors feel angry with God. This anger sometimes conflicts with survivors' feelings about "providence" or the concept that all things happen for a purpose. The middle-aged wife of a man who shot himself described her belief in God's providence: "I loved my husband very much. At first it was hard to accept but as I told my four year old (two and a half at the time), 'Daddy is with God in heaven and won't be back'—it became easier, knowing that everything happens for a purpose and God is a loving God." A forty-five-year-old man whose wife died of cancer put it this way: "I think God must have foreseen something in the future that must not have been good for us. I think it must have been God's will that this should happen, and that's the way I think I've looked at it. He must have done it for a purpose . . . it must have been the Lord's will or it wouldn't have happened."

On the other hand, some survivors feel more bitter about what they consider to be God's "providence" or lack of it. One reported, "I envy people who honestly have faith in God and can really gain strength through religion. My agonized prayers for the lives of my mother and husband went seemingly unheard. And then upon their deaths, my fervent prayers for comfort, strength, and stronger faith or anything that God could give me, which I so desperately needed to believe, also went unheard. I feel that if there is a God, he has nothing for me." These are the sad and bitter words of one who does not sense the love and comfort of God in her period of grief. God for her is not the Good Shepherd looking after his sheep, but a distant, mechanical "prime mover."

An interesting result of one of the statistical procedures (the factor analysis) was that questions related to suicide were highly related to questions dealing with a person's religious beliefs. This seems to suggest that suicide is more of a religious question than many mental health professionals have considered it to be. To elaborate further: suicidologists often do not see suicide to be as strongly laden with religious meaning in the eyes of the general public as it appears to be. Traditionally, suicide was considered a strictly religious and moral question, and the church throughout history has made pronouncements about suicide.[6] In recent years, however, suicide has been studied more as a mental health problem than as a religious problem. The tendency has been for mental health professionals who are untrained in theology to discount an individual's religious beliefs about suicide. I believe that the pendulum has swung too far, from an earlier dealing with suicide exclusively as a religious problem, to treating it almost totally as a mental health problem and neglecting the religious questions.

If this analysis is correct, it is important for the minister to use his unique training in theology and his unique role as a religious figure to aid suicide survivors in dealing with the guilt they feel. It is hypothesized that beneath the guilt of many suicide survivors is a feeling that one has somehow acted contrary to the will of God as well as against the deceased.

Meaning in Life

The open-ended question, "Who or what gives you meaning in life?" elicited one dominant statistic: 74% of both suicide and non-suicide survivors who responded listed their children. No other answer came close to this frequency; responses of work, "myself," life itself, God or the church, and new spouse or fiancé, were all clustered together as the second choice. There were no significant differences between suicide and non-suicide survivors regarding meaning in life.

Three things gave Mr. Dickinson meaning in life: "My kids . . . the girl I'm going to marry, and then taking a bigger interest in the church." He continued, "The fact that I have a relationship with her [his fiancée] is evidence to me that I can go on, the fact that she'd think as much as she does of me pleases me immensely, and my kids and my responsibility to them—I love them and I know they love me."

The sudden shock of death causes close survivors to reevaluate their lives to some extent. Several indicated some fairly significant reordering of priorities and values. This occurs especially among the young and middle-aged. One individual described his change of attitude toward life in this way: "I feel I'm a better-adjusted person than I was before. I think I understand a little more about what life is all about, what to look for in life. Before I had different ideas. . . . The death of my wife gave me a chance to sit back and maybe take stock of myself . . . I think it was a question of where do we go from here. What are we going to do now. Let's start making some plans."

For others who do not adapt well to the grief but are "stuck" in their mourning process, life lacks meaning and purpose. The Czechoslovakian immigrant referred to earlier described his feelings about life: "I would like to die today, not tomorrow. That's all. Because I have no reason to be alive. Even my son don't give me any more reason, because he is very selfish now, and he change so much. Why should I live? Why should I work? I am going to work every day but I don't know why. I don't know. Sometimes I ask myself . . . I ask him [God] please take me away, because it's no reason for my life." This man, forgotten by his friends and his church a year and a half after his wife's death, now sees his last thread of meaning in life—his son—being cut from him. This is a sad example of an unadaptive grief. How much better it would have been if someone had encountered this individual and known how to deal adequately with grief reactions so that he could have been helped, rather than wasting away in a meaningless life, praying each night that he will die.

Children

When someone dies, friends and relatives rally around the surviving parent but frequently give limited attention to the children. Words of comfort are directed to the children, but people usually do not ask them how they feel, if they know how the parent died, etc. The surviving parents, friends, and relatives all appear to assume that the deepest grief is felt by the parent—that the children are sad too, but they do not suffer as much. This popular assumption has never been validated. Dorpat, Cain and Fast, and others have indicated that the problem of grief is greater for the children than we commonly think, especially in cases of troubling deaths such as suicide. When this author interviewed surviving spouses, none of them knew how their children reacted to the death. They had never really talked to their children about it.

In the answers of survivors there appeared to be three ways in which children acted out their grief behaviorally. The first was physical illness. One housewife described her eighteen-year-old daughter's reaction: "This is something else that occurred about two weeks after my husband died. She became very ill. But before she had complained about feeling dizzy and nauseated at times and so about two weeks after he passed away she really became ill, and so I took her to a doctor, and through tests and everything found out that she is a diabetic." It appears, although the daughter may have shown some early signs of diabetes before, that the shock of her father's death so upset her body's equilibrium that the diabetes became evident. Several other parents said their children had a rash of colds, flu, upset stomachs, etc., for a few months after the death.

The second type of behavioral reaction was for the child to try to take the place of the deceased. One junior high school daughter almost completely took over her mother's duties. When her father started to come out of the shock of grief himself he realized what was occurring. "One thing that happened which in the long run made it a little bit more difficult for my daughter to adjust and gave me more problems was the fact so many people at the funeral . . . came up with the business of, 'Oh, you're the lady of the house, you have to take care of your daddy'—and this really led to a lot of problems, because she at the age of eleven or twelve assumed that she was just like my wife again. She was taking her place in every way possible. She did her damnedest to cook meals, keep the house straightened up, even assuming some of the habits of her mother in cleaning the house, ways of doing the house, things that she'd never done before. . . . And she took over a wife's role as much as a child could possibly do. . . . This went on I'd say for just about a year pretty consistently. I finally realized what was happening and that she was becoming so closely attached to me that I realized I had to do something about it. I started breaking away from her, doing more and more of those things myself, which made it hard for me too, but I think in the long run it was the best thing."

The third type of acting-out among children was to become "problem children." Mr. Dickinson's son in high school was very troubled by his mother's death, and within six months went from being an "A" student to "flunking out" and drifting aimlessly around the country—Bob didn't even know where he was at the time of the interview. Other parents also indicated that their children had difficulty in school. Several described the children as either "acting up" or having difficulty "concentrating." One mother related that several weeks after her husband died her six-year-old started stealing money. "I think he felt the death more than any of the kids. . . . And he started taking things, and the funny thing is he'd lay it where all the other kids would see it so they'd know to tell . . . like six or seven dollars he'd taken in and put on his dresser with the ends sticking out under the book. . . . The first time I talked to him I talked [logically] . . . the second time I threatened that if he ever did it again I was going to beat him within an inch of his life. So the next time when he did it I took him in the bedroom and I took his pants down and I said, 'Do you know what you're going to get?' He said, 'You're going to whip me, aren't you?' and he kind of had a smile on his face. I whipped the living daylights out of him and he hasn't done it again. I think he wanted to be punished. Because I imagine he felt responsible in some way . . . after I whipped the living daylights out of him he seemed happy as heck . . . I didn't have a problem." It appears from her description that the boy felt in some

53

way responsible for the suicide of his father and the spanking was to him a purging of his guilt.

Cain and Fast, in their study of the impact of parent suicide upon children, indicate that in the children studied there were highly individual reactions to the death, yet two factors seem to be most common. First, like adults, children experience quite a bit of guilt. Cain and Fast indicate that ". . . the severity of their guilt . . . took many forms: depression, masochistic character formation, guilt-laden obsessive ideation, externalization of a harsh superego, self-destructiveness, reactive ultra-goodness."[7] They found that the children frequently believed they were to a large extent responsible for the situation which ultimately led to suicide. ". . . the child was convinced that it was his basic badness or his father's disappointment in him that bred unhappiness and ultimately suicide; or he blamed himself for a good share of the marriage difficulties, for consistently siding against the suicide parent in arguments, for 'costing too much' amidst financial troubles, and he especially recalled parental arguments about himself."[8]

Children also felt they could have stopped the suicide act—if only they had not been away at camp, or if only they came home sooner from a friend's home. Others condemned themselves for not telling someone about the deceased's previous suicide attempts or mention of suicide to the child. This is important—many parents who commit suicide let their children know in some way that they are going to do it.

To this we can add the generally recognized desire of the child to make his parent disappear when he is not happy with him. Children who are angry with a parent will frequently wish he were dead and may even verbalize it: "I wish you were dead," "I want to kill you." Young children do not have an adult concept of death; what they are really saying is that they wish Mommy or Daddy would vanish for a few hours, at least until supper time. Death is not so final. The crisis occurs when the child begins to realize that Mommy is not coming back to cook supper. It intensifies when he thinks he caused her to go. It intensifies even more in suicide situations where the child believes he *made* Mommy kill herself.

The second important effect of the suicide death on children, according to Cain and Fast, is the distortion or avoidance of direct communication with the surviving parent. This occurs when the parent does not tell the children that their mother or father committed suicide. The children clearly receive the message that they are not to know about the suicide and that it is not to be discussed. In the Cain and Fast study, quite often the children knew about the suicide, sometimes even the most intimate details. About one-fourth of the children studied had directly witnessed some aspect of the suicide, yet the surviving parent told them that "Daddy died from a heart attack," etc. One girl saw her father's body hanging in a closet, but she was told that he died in an automobile accident.

In the present research, the wife of a man who hung himself didn't think her seven-year-old daughter knew he had committed suicide until six months later, when "I just looked at her and I said, You know how Daddy died? and she said, Well, I knew he killed himself, but I'm not exactly sure how—I heard things, and I said, What did you hear, and she said I heard he killed himself out in the garage with a rope, and I said, Yeah, that's right, he hung himself, it's like in a western, and she said, Well, he said he was going to do that. And I said, What do you mean, he said that, and she said, Oh, one night when you were gone shopping and he was mad at you about something . . . we were watching a western, and they hung a man, and he says that's the way you do it, with a new rope. And she says, Did he use a new rope, Mama? and I said, I don't know. And that was the end of the conversation."

A lack or distortion of communication has many problems for the children. "For the child, knowing and communicating become dangerous; his own projective distortions spring to the fore; he vacillates between grossly contradictory alternative beliefs and fantasies about his parent's death with specific constellations of defenses often forming around each of these fantasies."[9] Thus the child not only loses the opportunity to openly deal with his feelings, especially his guilt about the death, and reality-test his fantasies, but he also begins to feel it is dangerous to "know" or "communicate." Learning and knowing now can become a problem for the child. This can be exhibited in school behavior.

Parental Responsibility

The double responsibility of being both mother and father to the children who were left behind was more difficult than most people anticipated. Most of the surviving spouses interviewed (both suicide and non-suicide) said this double responsibility kept them so busy that they had little time for other activities. One woman said, "Your life naturally I think does change a little bit. You have more responsibilities. You've got all the grocery shopping to do, you've got all the checks to make out, and bills; if anything comes up you have to go and see about it yourself—so it did change in this respect because the man of the house was gone. He is no longer around the house to take care of things for you. If anything goes wrong with my car I've got to look around and find a dependable mechanic that will fix it nice, and, well, I guess it makes you feel stronger because these things have to be done, and you have to do them, so you go ahead and do them."

The man's point of view is much the same, but with different problems. "The hard thing is to be a mother and a father to a daughter, things like going shopping for clothes, making sure that she had the right clothes, yet you don't want to go overboard and get too many clothes. But what do you do? The Parent-Teachers call for a dozen cookies—that type of thing. It's pretty hard to fill a mother's role. You can't give the same type of companionship that a mother can; there's just no two ways about it; it's a difficult role to play."

A woman who had been having some difficulty adapting to the grief commented, "The children seem harder to deal with only because I feel so unsure of my own decisions regarding them. I always feel a deep need to talk things over with him." This points out the potential danger (whether or not the death was by suicide) that the surviving parent who is having trouble adapting to the loss may be irresponsible in child-rearing by not accepting the hard reality that the children are now totally in his or her hands. Unless the surviving parent adapts to this situation he or she is bound to have considerable difficulty at home.

Relations with the Opposite Sex and Remarriage

People who had been married for a number of years said they had some difficulty in relating to the opposite sex. Men especially experienced this, which may be in part because the man generally is expected to be the aggressor in American courting and sexual practices. The men in this study feared they would trip all over their feet as they began to relate to other women again. They did not know how to meet women on a courting or dating basis after being deeply involved in a marriage relationship. A man told of one of his first outings: "I found it very hard to talk to people . . . I didn't want to dance; I didn't feel in the mood for it. It was a very hard thing. I left very early. . . . I think it was a fear of new people, what are you going to say, you know. You've been married for twenty years and you've been used to the actions and reactions of a certain woman. Now how do you talk to somebody else. Fortunately, or unfortunately, I never chased another woman, so I felt that I'd lost the magical charm, the touch, the old line of baloney that you needed, and I found I felt lost. I tell you, it was hard . . . I was just afraid I would make a fool of myself, not to know what to say, not to be able to talk."

The fear of impotence is very real for these middle-aged, middle-class men. One described his struggles: ". . . the first two or three women I dated or tried to screw, I couldn't pull it off. That's what I really feared very much, was being impotent. Well, fortunately with this one woman I found out I was not impotent, certainly. And that was of tremendous importance to me . . . to know you can make it with a woman, because I had serious doubts whether I ever would." This man said that he still felt loyal to his deceased wife—so loyal that he was impotent at first. For a while after the death he felt that he would never be able to have intercourse with a woman again. Describing his relationship with the last woman he said, "She helped me to realize I could still attract a woman and increased my sense of self-worth." The men who were successfully able to relate interpersonally and/or sexually with a woman they cared about sensed a massive boost in their self-esteem and their feelings of manliness.

One of the major factors keeping several individuals from remarriage was the fear of losing another spouse and going through the grief all over again. One woman described her feelings: "I'll never forget it [the death of her husband]. I would think 40,000 times before marrying again, because of . . . the terror of ever losing so badly again, and so painfully. . . . I think you need a lot of time to be open enough to start to love . . . it's a question of adjusting to opening up enough to get yourself that vulnerable again. The scar tissue isn't even healed yet."

The spouses (suicide or non-suicide) who remarried generally adapted to their grief better than those who remained single. This may imply either that those who marry again have done a good job of accepting the death of their former spouse and thus feel free to marry again, or it may mean that the process of remarrying and loving another person furthers the acceptance of the loss. I believe both are true. In other words, an individual is more likely to consider loving another if he has severed his former relationship with the deceased, and at the same time the act of marrying again—of giving oneself again in love to another—is very helpful to the grief process. As one woman said, "A close friend introduced me to a wonderful man that took my five children and me out and helped us get over our sorrow."

When I began to research the suicide grief I anticipated that the surviving spouse of a suicide would be more reticent to remarry. This is not the case. There appears to be no difference in the percentage of remarriage between suicide and non-suicide spouses. Also, those suicide survivors who remarried were adapting to the loss of their previous mates just as well as the non-suicide surviving spouses; there is no difference between suicide and non-suicide survivors in this respect.

Social Involvement and the Use of Resources

I asked suicide and non-suicide survivors, "Circle any of the following which were very helpful in aiding you to adjust to your spouse's death" (followed by a list of common resources).[10] (See Appendix B.) About two-thirds listed children and close friends. Next in order of importance were relatives. Prayer and Bible reading were helpful to 27%, and their minister and church were helpful to 21% and 18% respectively. Of the traditional medical and mental health professionals, only the family doctor seems to have been much help. Counselors or psychotherapists, social workers, and other professionals helped only three individuals. Except for the family doctor, the minister was the only professional important in aiding grief sufferers. Both suicide and non-suicide survivors appear the same in their utilization of resources. Although they were helped by their close friends, suicide and non-suicide survivors reported a significant changeover of friends. In other words, they lost many old friends, but those who adapted well to the grief created a new group of friends. One widow related, "Your friends try to include you as before, but it just isn't the same, you feel like a fifth wheel and the relationship is not as it used to be, no matter how hard you try." Another said,

"I still miss her [his wife] occasionally. I guess other people do too, but the main reason they don't is because I've sort of changed my circle of friends . . . not that I've lost all my old friends, I just don't have as much in common with them that I had before. . . . It's fine to visit people who are couples, it's nice to be invited over for dinner. It isn't nice to have them try to make matches for you by inviting an extra woman along. I had to drop some good friends . . . because every time I was invited to dinner there was always an attractive young widow or divorcée with five or ten kids or what have you. . . . For another thing, I had maybe more time with one particular friend because his wife and my wife were very close and we were close. I was close to his wife as a good friend . . . but when word filtered back to me, as it usually does, that he felt I was trying to take his wife away from him, I was dropped. Just quite completely . . . I got more pushed out of shape I think by that than anything that happened, that some other guy would think I wanted his wife. . . . After this one thing happened I think I became overly cautious about that."

The change of friends seems to occur because (1) the individual is now single and most couples like to do things with other couples; (2) the single individual is suspected of seeking out other husbands or wives; (3) some friends were more attracted to the deceased spouse and not the survivor, and consequently fell away; and (4) in an effort to meet other people to date, the survivor spends more and more time with new groups of people and has less time for old friends. These points are summed up by the Czechoslovakian immigrant referred to earlier. He had not created new friendships to speak of and was very lonely. He described his feelings this way: "But you know friends when you are married—good time, coming everybody. But when you alone, nobody open your door . . . because everybody is married, and people think if they coming something happen because I am alone. You know people. But I never was such a man. I never looking for other man's wife. I never want to, even to other man's wife . . . I looking for a good woman I would like to marry, but I don't want some junk."

Summary

In this chapter several factors peripheral to the basic dynamics of the grief reaction, but a part of the total pattern of grief, have been discussed. As indications of the grief response of an individual, these are not as crucial as those found in the last chapter, but they should have helped to give the reader a more complete picture of the grief response. There are fewer differences between the suicide and non-suicide survivors than were noted in the last chapter. Nevertheless, three crucial differences should be noted.

In the first place, we saw that individuals who are college-educated generally adapt better to the loss of a loved one than those who are not as well educated. The exception is that the suicide spouse is not better off for being college-educated. This means that to the person with a college education, the shock of suicide strikes with more fury than to the non-suicide college-educated person.

A second difference between suicide and non-suicide survivors occurs in a child's reaction to the suicide. Intense feelings of guilt, and distorted or missing communication with the surviving parent, are what distinguish him from children who have lost a parent by natural causes.

A final result was that Roman Catholic suicide spouses experience considerably more guilt than Roman Catholic or Protestant non-suicide survivors, or even Protestant suicide survivors. This seems to stem historically from the Roman Church's strong moral stand against suicide. It will be interesting to note if this difference continues in the future, as the effects of Vatican II change the attitudes of the laity toward the authority of the Church.

NOTES

1. Edgar Jackson, *Understanding Grief* (New York: Abingdon Press, 1957), pp. 41–42; and Mervyn Shoor and Mary H. Speed, "Death, Delinquency and the Mourning Process," in *Death and Identity,* ed. Robert Fulton (New York: John Wiley & Sons, Inc., 1965), pp. 201–16.

2. Jackson, *Understanding Grief,* p. 42.

3. See pp. 52–55.

4. Jackson, *Understanding Grief,* pp. 42–43.

5. See Appendix B.

6. See Paul Pretzel's "Suicide and Religion: A Preliminary Study" (Th.D. thesis, School of Theology at Claremont, Claremont, California, 1966).

7. Albert C. Cain and Irene Fast, "A Clinical Study of Some Aspects of the Psychological Impact of Parental Suicide Upon Children," *American Journal of Orthopsychiatry* XXXV:2 (1965): 319.

8. Albert C. Cain and Irene Fast, "Children's Disturbed Reaction to Parent Suicide," *American Journal of Orthopsychiatry* XXXVI:5 (1966): 877.

9. Cain and Fast, "A Clinical Study of Some Aspects of the Psychological Impact of Parental Suicide Upon Children," p. 319.

10. See Glossary for definition of resources.

5. PASTORAL CARE OF
THE SUICIDE SURVIVOR

Let us ask why it is that precisely in thoroughly grave situations, for instance when I am with someone who has suffered a bereavement, I often decide to adopt a "penultimate" attitude . . . remaining silent as a sign that I share in the bereaved man's helplessness in the face of such a grievous event, and not speaking the Biblical words of comfort which are, in fact, known to me and available to me. Why am I often unable to open my mouth, when I ought to give expression to the ultimate? And why, instead, do I decide on an expression of thoroughly penultimate human solidarity? Is it from mistrust of the power of the ultimate word? Is it from fear of men? Or is there some good positive reason for such an attitude, namely, that my knowledge of the word, my having it at my finger-tips, in other words my being, so to speak, spiritually master of the situation, bears only the appearance of the ultimate, but is in reality itself something entirely penultimate? *Does one not in some cases, by remaining deliberately in the penultimate, perhaps point all the more genuinely to the ultimate,* which God will speak in His own time. . . . Does not this mean that, over and over again, the penultimate will be what commends itself precisely for the sake of the ultimate, and that it will have to be done not with a heavy conscience but with a clear one? . . . [This question] embraces the whole domain of Christian social life, and especially the whole range of Christian pastoral activity.[1] (Italics mine.)

The Task of Pastoral Care

This struggle with what to do and say when you are faced with a bereaved individual, which Bonhoeffer has so aptly expressed, is the one to which we shall address ourselves presently. As a pastoral counselor, I view a wide variety of personal problems as being essentially religious. As a rule, though, I do not try to approach them in an "ultimate" way (the ultimate for Bonhoeffer is the justification of man by God alone). When I say that personal problems are religious at their core, I mean they involve religious questions on which an individual needs to focus if his life is to be fulfilling.[2] In most cases what the survivor needs least is for the minister to preach at him about ultimate issues such as God's grace and his salvation. Doing so may be a minister's sincere attempt to operate within the sphere of the ultimate, but most likely the ultimate word will actually *not* be spoken because he is not meeting the overarching human needs of the bereaved.

To act penultimately in a grief situation is to act in a human, responsive way toward the bereaved so that whatever you do will prepare the way for God to speak his ultimate word to the individual. Thus whether you stand in the "human solidarity" of which Bonhoeffer speaks, or use your skills and knowledge of psychology, or simply listen to the bereaved individual's recital of woes in the weeks and months that follow a death, you are ministering to that individual. Like Bonhoeffer, I believe that in such situations you are pointing to the ultimate word God speaks when he wills. In other words, ministers should not feel embarrassed to use their skills in pastoral counseling or their training in psychology when ministering to the grief-stricken. (The goal of such counseling is to foster the I-Thou, God-man encounter contextually i.e., each situation may require a different word or a different act.)

So far in this book I have sketched a background of grief and suicide and detailed some ways in which suicide survivors typically respond to their grief. This is only half the battle. Knowing the dynamics is necessary, but so is knowing methods of pastoral care in that situation. We realize that each bereaved person is different, yet there are some basic ways in which they all usually respond; likewise, there are some basic ways in which they can all be helped. The task of the present chapter is to present some ideas and suggestions as to how the bereaved can be aided in their grief process. It should be noted that all of these suggestions are dependent upon the minister's ability to develop rapport with people. In other words, a caring personal relationship with the bereaved is absolutely essential for any help to occur. I have a fear that someone reading this book without having a good grasp of this counseling relationship will turn it into a "bag of techniques"—a sort of do-it-yourself manual for counseling. The methods I am presenting are valuable, but *only* as building blocks on top of the minister's fundamental ability to develop rapport with his parishioner, to give him an idea of ways in which he can foster and encourage this relationship.

On the other hand, there are many books in psychotherapy and pastoral counseling which tell the minister what the counseling relationship is to be like, but do not give the slightest hint as to how to develop this relationship or what might be more or less helpful counseling methods. I would suggest that anyone who has not done much reading in the field of pastoral counseling and psychotherapy look at some of these books.[3]

With the foregoing cautions in mind, I should like to suggest in this chapter some ways in which the basic attitudes and concepts of the minister might be manifested (i.e., a pastoral relationship established) with the individual who is suffering from grief.

The Minister's Role

The pastor has several natural advantages in his ministry to the bereaved. It was noted in Chapter 4 that most people, both churched and unchurched, actually *expect* the minister to be present after a death. Since he is the one designated by society to deal with the deceased and their survivors, he can involve himself and the church immediately, and can continue his contact with the family long after the death. These unique advantages make him the ideal person to work therapeutically with the bereaved.

In this crucial period of bereavement people are open to the caring of the church. I stress this because an increasing number of ministers incorrectly assume that people no longer care much for being visited in their homes, and this belief spills over into their handling of such crises as bereavement. I believe they are missing a very rich opportunity by neglecting or playing down their pastoral care to the family of the deceased, who both need and want more than a coldly impersonal funeral. They need and frequently expect the minister's presence both before and after the funeral.

The individuals who participated in this research were asked to "Please write on these lines what a rabbi/minister/priest did that aided you in your time of grief." A few representative comments follow:

"[The] message before and during the funeral was from his heart and helped us all in our loss."

"Made me realize that perhaps all is not lost after all."

"I am very grateful to my church and fellow Christians for their love and understanding."

"Calm encouragement without being maudlin."
They were also asked to write what was not helpful.

"The minister was arranged for through the funeral parlor. He called me once and spoke to me briefly, too briefly. The service was too impersonal and too long. He could have been talking about anybody."

"No help, he only tried to convert me back to the church."

". . . minister said my husband was taken to punish me and he probably couldn't go to heaven because he had never been baptized."

Although there were some negative comments, the general feeling was either neutral or mildly positive toward the minister. There were no noticeable differences between suicide and non-suicide responses. It appears that what the bereaved (suicide and non-suicide alike) appreciated in the minister was a calm, steady acceptance of them. They wanted to experience that there was still hope, that there was still a reason for living. People in crisis are especially sensitive to phoniness; they appreciated the minister who "spoke from the heart." They did not like to be preached at, converted, told that their spouse's death was God punishing them for their sins, that the deceased would go to hell.

We who are ministers need to realize that pastoral care goes beyond what the pastor himself can say and do, to include how he can put friends, relatives, and other resources at the bereaved's disposal. Since the close friends and family of the bereaved are their greatest help during grief, part of the pastor's care to the survivors will be the help and encouragement he gives to these key individuals, who may be frightened and anxious about death—especially if it is a suicide. The minister's task is to work with their feelings so they can provide a firm system of support for the bereaved. This does not negate the importance of personal ministry to the close survivors; rather, I am suggesting that the ministry we share with the close friends and relatives of the bereaved may ultimately be the most effective form of pastoral care we can offer. This is most crucial with suicide survivors because the "double trouble" of death *and* suicide creates greater anxiety and avoidance tendencies in those close to the bereaved.

The Minister's Feelings about Death and Suicide

Friends and relatives will frequently let their anxiety keep them from becoming involved with the survivors following a suicide. Ministers can also be hindered by their anxiety from meeting the bereaved's needs. I am aware of several ministers who will not officiate at funerals because it makes them so emotionally distraught. Bachmann says, "In times of grief the pastor's own personality, feelings, or attitudes toward death, grief, and the grief sufferer will either handicap or enhance his ability to be a part of the helping process."[4] In a recent conversation with the author, a young pastor who had been in the ministry for ten years described the way he felt about funerals. In his first funerals he really became involved with the survivors of the deceased and spent a lot of time with them, and became so emotionally exhausted that he could do little else in the parish for several days. He did this for the first five years, especially the first two years, of his ministry and then decided to limit himself to officiating at the funeral, talking with the bereaved before and afterwards, but not getting involved as he had been doing. This minister feels, and I believe he is correct, that many other ministers have experienced the same thing. I believe they have not come to grips with questions of life and death, and are not at peace with themselves about their own death, and therefore are not able to minister well in grief situations.

Ministers who have not dealt with their feelings about a certain dynamic of the grief response (such as bitchiness in women survivors, or strong expressions of anger in men, etc.) either remain emotionally uninvolved, or they sympathize. Both reactions have disastrous consequences in counseling with the bereaved, and can also give the minister himself trouble emotionally.

I believe the emotional involvement needed is empathy rather than sympathy or noninvolvement. Sympathy gets us involved in a way that has us feeling all the feelings which the bereaved feel, as if we *were* the bereaved. We do not distinguish between ourselves and the people for whom we are caring. A simple example of this is a mother who feels pain in her arm after her child has fallen and cut his arm.

Empathy involves the minister sensing the feelings of the bereaved—and yet realizing that there is a distinction between himself and the bereaved. Empathy is not drawing away from the feelings (which would be noninvolvement), but rather daring to become involved and sense the feelings of the bereaved without letting these feelings overtake him or trigger his own unresolved feelings about death. Until the minister is willing to be aware of and deal with his feelings about death and suicide, he will tend to tip the balance toward either sympathy or noninvolvement.

The Crisis Period

An important element in pastoral care to the grieving is the age of the grief. A grief of only a few hours is handled differently from one six months old. When the minister encounters the suicide survivor a few hours after the death, the dynamics of shock and catharsis are prevalent, and the first questioning—"What did I do to make him do it?"—has begun.

It might be valuable at this point to describe theoretically what a crisis is, and to suggest its component parts.[5] A crisis can be divided into four basic aspects (see diagram). (a) The first is the stimulus of the crisis—the event. In the present discussion the precipitating event is the suicide of a close relative or friend. (b) Second is the individual's own perception of the event. Each person who has been close to the deceased will perceive the death in a unique way. His perception of the event is colored by his past experiences with the deceased, the depth of his involvement, his previous experiences of loss, and his own personality dynamics. How important the loss appears to the bereaved affects to a great extent whether or not it will become a crisis of great proportion. Thus the wife of the deceased who has been deeply involved in her husband's life will perceive a greater loss than will his business associates. (c) The third aspect of crisis is the individual's personal resources and coping abilities. Here all external and internal resources (e.g., abilities to face and cope with crises, and friends, relatives, institutions or organizations which an individual might draw upon for help in his grief) are used in coping with the survivor's perception of the event. The adequacy of these resources and coping abilities affects how much a stimulus will be experienced as crisis. (d) This all leads to the crisis, an individual's *internal reaction to an external hazard* (here, death by suicide). It is an acute disturbance resulting from the individual's perception of the emotionally hazardous situation.

Precipitating event ⟶ perception of the event ⟶ resources and coping abilities ⟶ crisis

---

To further describe what a crisis is, Taplin has made eight observations about crises:

(a) Life is a succession of crisis events which occur in the normal maturational-developmental-social learning process. (b) Crises have a definite course in time and in their quality of "upsetness." (c) Crises are more accessible to intervention at their peak and may be resolved in adaptive or maladaptive ways. A crisis is, in effect, a temporary state of psychological accessibility. (d) A history of successful crisis resolution increases the probability of a successful resolution of crises in the future. (e) Assistance in crisis does not have to come from specially skilled professionals; the humanity of significant others (resource persons) may be sufficient and necessary. (f) Situational aspects play an important part in sustaining the crisis. Changes of situation, sometimes called behavior setting, can significantly affect the course of a crisis. (g) The onset of crisis usually involves identifiable precipitators (event), generally of a situational or interpersonal nature. (h) Fulfillment of expectancies is related to beneficial interventive outcome.[6]

These observations are applicable to the crisis work after a suicide. The suicide ("identifiable precipitator" or "precipitating event") is a crisis which has a "definite course in time." The crisis following a suicide generally lasts a maximum of six weeks. The grief reaction is by no means over after six weeks; only the crisis is over at that time. By the end of four to six weeks the bereaved have pretty much developed the style that their grief reaction will take in the future.

It is important for the minister or counselor to realize that to a large extent the way an individual is going to adapt to his grief is formed during this crisis phase. The months and years that follow are a "living-out" of this style of reacting to the loss. This does not mean the minister has his hands tied after the crisis period is over, but it has two implications for him. First, any counseling which occurs after the crisis period will generally take more time because the state of heightened psychological accessibility is past. One way to explain this is to use Morley's diagram of a crisis.[7] In Diagram 1 the

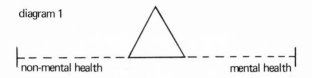

triangle represents an individual who is not in a crisis state. Morley would say he is in a "state of relative equilibrium." This state is maintained by means of a complicated network of relationships between the individual and significant persons in his environment. *For each person this relative equilibrium is located at a point on a continuum of mental health or lack of mental health.* By equilibrium I do not imply that the person is stuck within a status quo and is not in continual growth (this is where Morley's diagram breaks down). Rather I mean that a large part of each of us is stable and can be relied upon. To live normal lives we need a certain amount of personality stability; if we lack it we develop unadaptively.

The second implication of the brevity of the crisis period is emphasized by Taplin—the accessibility of the person who is in the crisis state.[8] Diagram 2 illustrates this. The individual indicated by

the triangle is in a state of crisis; his "triangle" is tipped on end. His relative state of equilibrium is broken and he is in a state of cognitive and emotional dissonance. The importance of this state of disequilibrium is that the individual wants to reestablish stability and leave the crisis state, and is therefore very susceptible to any influences from the outside which will aid him in resolving the crisis. With a minimal effort on the part of the minister, family members, or mental health professionals, a maximum amount of leverage may be exerted upon the individual. That is, during the period of crisis, with the individual's greater susceptibility to change, less counseling effort is required to aid him towards an adaptive resolution of his problems. The difficulty frequently is that we do not help soon enough. When the crisis stage is past, it takes considerably more leverage to bring change because the "triangle" is back on its base, as in Diagram 1.

People cannot live in a state of crisis or disequilibrium for very long, or they will become either physically sick—even unto death— or psychotic. As an example of this, Anderson made a study in a British hospital and found that 9% of its total admissions were there because of an unadaptive grief response to a recent loss.[9] They were not able to respond to their grief adaptively and so developed psychotic symptoms as a way of dealing with the extreme pain of their loss. Thus, counseling after the state of heightened accessibility has passed generally involves a greater investment of time and effort on the part of both client and minister.

The individual who successfully resolves a crisis can emerge a healthier person than he was before the crisis. Most readers will have experienced this personally, or known someone who has, for example, a person who has been in the hospital and has described his stay as a meaningful learning experience. He would not want to do it over again but he feels and changed, sees life differently.

But the opposite can occur as well. Some who are reading this book have also known individuals who never recovered from the death of their spouse and have gone around under a cloud for years, with little purpose or meaning left in life. They have responded to their crisis unadaptively. Thus a motto of crisis theory is, "A crisis is both a danger and an opportunity." When a person is in a state of disequilibrium he can move towards greater health in his adaption to the grief, or he can move away from mental health. Which way he will go is dependent partially upon the response of his friends, relatives, and others (including the minister) who express their caring or lack of caring for him.

Ministering to the Bereaved in Crisis

When the minister first hears of a death, his initial contact with the survivor is crucial. The bereaved needs someone who in a quiet, calm, and stable way will let him know he cares and is there to help in any way he is able. The strength of the minister, as one who has lived through the griefs of others, can be appropriated to some extent by the survivor. In a growing number of cases families will have talked together ahead of time about what they are going to do when one of them dies, regarding burial, funeral, care of children, finances, etc.—but, more frequently they will not have discussed it and will benefit by the minister's willingness to guide them, suggesting alternative ways of dealing with their immediate problems. He should avoid making decisions for the survivors, however.

The minister also needs to realize that during the crisis the bereaved may be irritable or downright angry—especially at those who were near to him at the time of death. He will also frequently be angry at God and at persons he views as God's representatives (ministers). Therefore a pastor may face a barrage of subtle or overt anger in the first few days and sometimes for months to follow. It is important not to be scared away by it. The pastor who sees himself as a "nice guy" may be offended by such outbursts and retreat, just when the grieving person needs him most. In the case of a suicide where the minister had been counseling the deceased, the survivors may aim a lot of their anger and blame at him and he must be prepared to handle it.

For the first few hours after the death until the funeral, it is important for the minister to be as accepting as he can of whatever the bereaved is feeling. He is there as a resource person, making suggestions and discussing alternatives for immediate action without actually doing everything for the survivors. The minister also needs to respect the bereaved's wishes for time alone to reflect on what has happened and to become aware of his feelings. Several individuals have indicated that they had difficulty getting time alone in the first four or five days after their spouses' death. Friends, in an effort to help, besieged them with telephone calls and visits. Some of this was helpful, but they also needed time to be alone and reflect on the dramatic change in their lives. They related that what was most helpful was for one trusted individual (friend, relative, minister) to just be with them, not saying anything unless the bereaved wanted to talk. In this way the survivor could appropriate the strength of this individual and be alone with his or her thoughts, without being isolated.

Sympathy at this time is not helpful; it only makes the individual feel more depressed and helpless. Of both suicide and non-suicide survivors, 39% responded to the following statement in the affirmative: "After a while I got tired of people always trying to console me about my spouse's death." Poems and cards, and hundreds of "you have my deepest sympathies," were appreciated by some but to others it was irritating. What seemed to trigger this irritation was "phoniness" or formality, instead of genuine personal concern.

A week or two after the funeral, when most of the relatives have gone home, is a very hard time for the survivor. Most of his friends and relatives are back to "business as usual," but he is still feeling very lost and confused. The minister can express his concern at this time, without giving "sympathy," by helping the individual to begin facing reality and his present responsibilities, and to solve his immediate and short-range problems. Discussing alternatives (without making the decisions) and gently nudging the bereaved into action may be necessary. In the first few weeks it is most helpful for the bereaved to be able to complete successfully small, specific tasks. If he tries to tackle too many or too difficult tasks and fails, he will feel even more helpless and depressed. These small early successes form a foundation upon which increasingly difficult tasks can follow.

Warren Jones, a psychiatrist, has developed a model of crisis intervention counseling,[10] the "ABC" method which is viable for the pastoral care and counseling of suicide survivors.[11] It is somewhat different from the two major styles of pastoral counseling which have been prevalent in this century. The first of these is what I call the authoritarian model. It involves the minister as an authority figure telling the parishioner what he should do to solve his problem (a deteriorating marriage, for example). This method is not very helpful in that the minister will tell the couple with the marriage problem what he thinks they ought to do without listening much to their feelings or for the dynamics of the problem. The authoritarian model has frequently been little more than shallow advice-giving. Its advantages are that it takes little of the minister's precious time, and that it focuses directly on problem-solving and behavior change (I will return to this latter point).

The second main style of pastoral counseling in this century, nondirective counseling, has influenced pastoral counseling theory since the early 1940s. It has taught the minister to listen in depth to the feelings as well as the words of his parishioner, and to focus on the basic dynamics of the problem rather than only on surface symptoms, a needed change in pastoral counseling. It has also brought problems. Under the nondirective influence, much of pastoral counseling has focused on feeling, catharsis, "getting it all out," and minimized helping people to change their behavior on the assumption that behavioral change will follow naturally, when in actuality this does not always occur. A second problem to the minister—who sees far more individuals in crisis than do most mental health professionals—is that the nondirective model is not short-term and based on crisis theory, but rather one which is used more by psychiatrists and psychologists who do considerably more long-term therapy than he has time for. Thus the nondirective model of counseling does not fit well with the minister's clientele or his schedule.

Crisis intervention counseling aims at utilizing the advantages of both of the above approaches, yet avoiding their pitfalls. It does not shy away from legitimate use of authority; at times the crisis counselor will give advice or help the individual with tasks (e.g., job hunting, renting an apartment, writing a letter, etc.) which the ordinary counselor might not do. He also focuses on problem-solving and changing behavior, on making decisions and carrying them out. All this he does without ignoring feelings or the dynamics of the individual's problem; but he realizes that, as Karl Menninger once said, "You don't have to know how a fire started to put it out."[12] It is not necessary to understand all the intricate dynamics of the suicide survivor's past in order to help him deal with present grief.

The "ABC" method of crisis intervention counseling adapted here follows three basic steps.

A. The first task of the minister is to *achieve contact*. This simply means establishing a therapeutic relationship with the bereaved traditionally referred to as "rapport." The relationship may already exist for the minister if the bereaved are members of his congregation and he has aided them in some of their normal developmental crises (birth, marriage, etc.). Achieving contact occurs through the minister becoming actively involved with the bereaved. This means (1) listening and asking questions that focus on his feelings as well as his behavior, and (2) letting him know you care about him, that you are willing to listen to the feelings he is experiencing and are not frightened away by them. The calm, yet concerned response of the minister which I spoke of earlier in relation to the initial contacts with the bereaved is very essential. It furthers the development of a relationship which is invaluable to the survivor in the present, and is also ready for him to fall back upon in the future. If the bereaved does not trust the minister or sense a relationship at this early stage in the grief, there is little hope that at a later time the minister will be able to help him.[13]

Thus, the success or failure of crisis intervention counseling rests largely on the minister's ability to achieve human contact with the bereaved and develop a relationship with him.[14] The most important aspect of this relationship is Christian love, which involves a respect for the other person, a desire to know him better, positive feelings for him, and a giving and sharing of yourself with him. These elements in the minister-parishioner relationship provide a firm basis for focusing openly and honestly on critical problems.

A second aspect of the relationship is a sense of human equality. The minister may know more about theology and counseling, but he and his client are very much equal as human beings encountering each other. It is essential that the client sense this equality of personhood or there will be a tendency for him to become infantilized in the face of the knowledgeable minister or counselor, further immobilizing his already shaky coping abilities.

A third quality of the relationship is presence. Although the minister is on the one hand a professional person doing his job as minister to the bereaved, he also needs to be vitally present in the relationship as a human being. The minister can help the bereaved to sense this presence by being empathic and responsive, interested, concerned, attentive, and nonpunitive.

In this relationship it is essential to affirm the infinite worth of the bereaved. In Buber's phrase, an "I-Thou" relationship exists in which healing can and will occur.

B. The second step in the "ABC" model of crisis intervention counseling is *boiling down*. This involves focusing the feelings of the bereaved, helping him to move away from the amorphous mass of his grief where he can't understand what has happened to him, to a point where he can define in his own mind what has happened and what he is actually feeling. This is important because grief is a composite of several strong feelings (depression, anger, guilt, etc.).[15] In grief, individuals have feelings they haven't felt for a long time (or haven't felt to such a great degree), and as a result they sense that they are in the clutches of their feelings and cannot extricate themselves.

Focusing on the components of the problem—what is bothering them most and what they have tried to do about it—is helpful in itself. It accomplishes a basic purpose of crisis counseling, which is to help a person pull out of his tailspin. We do not necessarily have to peer into the dim, dark past of the person to discover why he is having difficulty coping with his grief. Often it is enough that in the boiling down and focusing process the individual has been helped to come out of his tailspin and begin to think clearly, sort out his feelings, and begin to do something about his crisis. This in itself enhances his self-esteem.

C. The final stage of the "ABC" model of crisis intervention counseling is *challenging the person to cope*. At this point the minister helps the bereaved to actually do something about his situation, to cope actively with his grief. One of the worst things that a grieving person can do is to isolate himself in his room, let someone do everything for him, and just sit waiting for the grief to pass—doing so will often lead to long bouts with depression and self-pity. As long as an individual simply talks about his grief and does not do anything, he will not gain maximum strength in recovering from whatever it is that is paralyzing his inner resources. And so the pastor helps the suicide survivor to examine what alternative courses of action he can take to reshape his life without the deceased, and then challenges him to act upon these alternatives.

Clinebell has emphasized the importance of getting a person into action.[16] He compares an individual's personality or self to a muscle. When you use a muscle it grows stronger; if you don't use the muscle it begins to atrophy or waste away. Likewise the person who is in the crisis of grief—his personality and self-esteem will grow stronger as he exercises them. Many individuals in grief quite naturally begin to reevaluate their lives, where they are going to go from here, and begin to act on their reevaluation. With such individuals the minister need only stand by ready to help if needed. Let us not forget that there are many individuals who have good resources and need little help from the minister in adapting well to their grief. Clinebell says, "The minister's role in normal grief is to cooperate with the psyche's built-in recovery forces."[17] The minister's job is to become involved only when necessary, and also to be aware if any signs of a potentially unadaptive grief are present. If the minister sees, for example, that an individual is not "catharting" but rather putting a lid down hard on his feelings, he must intervene before it becomes a fixed style of adapting to the grief. At the end of this chapter I will suggest some indicators of a possible unadaptive grief which the pastor can look for.

There are many obvious similarities between the "ABC" method of crisis intervention counseling and other more traditional forms of counseling. It may be helpful at this point to summarize several of the differences.

Crisis intervention counseling is based upon the theory of the components of a crisis—e.g., how a crisis occurs and develops, heightened accessibility, and so forth. A second difference is that crisis counseling is *supportive* therapy, rather than *uncovering* as in psychoanalysis. Its goal is not to break down defense mechanisms but rather to build upon the client's existing strengths and resources.

Crisis counseling is almost by definition short-term and is not a suggested procedure for long-term counseling. It is viable for up to six weeks, the usual maximum duration of a crisis. This form of counseling is present-oriented, focusing on the here and now, on specific and concrete problems. Although the crisis counselor may see other problems which an individual needs to deal with, he focuses only on the special problems related to the crisis. For example: a minister, confronted with a husband and wife who have lost their seventeen-year-old son by suicidal drug overdose, is aware that they are experiencing serious marital problems, but he will not focus on their marriage problems until he has helped them work through the crisis of their grief.

The term "crisis intervention *counseling*" may sometimes be a misnomer because it frequently falls within what is known as *pastoral care*. In other words, it involves much more than fifty-minute weekly sessions; it tends to be less structured than other forms of counseling and adapts itself to the best ways of serving the needs of each individual. Thus, much of a minister's crisis intervention work with the bereaved is done in hospital corridors, in back rooms of funeral parlors, or over a cup of tea in the bereaved's living room.

Crisis intervention counseling is also action-oriented. By this I mean it does not focus much on reflecting feelings, as does nondirective counseling, but rather upon helping people to *do something* about their problems.[18]

A final distinction between crisis counseling and other forms of counseling is that it attempts to involve the largest available system of resources and the greatest possible number of people who are significant to the bereaved. It is thus not simply a one-to-one relationship between the minister and the bereaved. Part of its focus is also upon helping other people, friends and relatives, to minister to the survivors effectively themselves.

The Funeral and the Funeral Service

Death is always hard. Sudden death finds us unprepared, and death by suicide is perhaps the most difficult to accept. Not only do the survivors have to adapt to the death itself and learn to accept the fact that it was a suicide; they may also struggle with the question of whether a person who commits suicide can ever go to heaven. The funeral service is not the time to answer all of the questioning of the survivors or to act as an apologist for the suicide victim, though the minister cannot pretend that these questions and feelings do not exist. Most counseling and pastoral care with suicide survivors must be done individually, but the funeral service can be a time when that care is highlighted. As much openness concerning the suicide as the survivors can take is appropriate and necessary. The minister, in a caring way, should deal honestly with the feelings of the survivors concerning the suicide, realizing that some are not ready to deal with it at this time. Above all the funeral can never take the place of his individual pastoral care and counseling with the survivors.

The following question about the funeral was asked of spouses who had quite recently lost their mates: "Please write on the back what in the funeral helped you and what did not." Below are a few of the varied responses to the question.

"The funeral did make me feel better . . . seeing how nice he looked and so very peaceful, I felt slightly relieved."

"I do not feel that the funeral helped me in any way. I was in a state of shock at the time. It was as if it weren't happening to me."

"The funeral home and priest were very helpful. The costs of the funeral and burial were too high."

"I think the funeral was more depressing. I feel they should be abolished completely."

"Over three hundred people came to his funeral. This made the children and I feel pretty proud."

". . . I consider them a barbaric custom, but it is difficult to fly in the face of generally accepted custom. . . . The only good at all was seeing family and friends and absorbing their sympathy and understanding."

"I realized that I would now have to make a new life."

"It was a tribelike ritual, and even though it was closed-coffin, the smell of the flowers, and the smell and look of grief was the most macabre and nauseous experience I've had. The experience clings around one like a musty drape, and death I can cope with, the capitalization I cannot."

Most individuals responding to the question were neutral about the value of the funeral. Only 9% felt it was very helpful in their adjustment to the loss. It seemed comforting to a few and a gaudy, costly, senseless ritual to a few others. There were no differences between the suicide and non-suicide responses.

There is much upheaval in funeral practices today. A few people, especially some in the funeral industry, would like to make the funeral an even more elaborate, gaudy, painted-face affair than it already is. In contrast, other people suggest that we do away with funerals altogether. I cannot align myself with either pole, yet the present research indicates that funeral practices are not as effective as they should be—neither as "grief therapy" (a funeral industry term) nor in proclaiming the hope and realities of the gospel. Robert Fulton, a sociologist, in a study of 633 clergymen, found that 51% of the Protestants and 41% of the Roman Catholics believed the undertaker exploits rather than helps a family's grief.[19] Carl Wennerstrom, former chaplain of the University of Chicago Hospitals, says, "In the course of my ministry, I constantly see families being victimized financially and emotionally, at the time of death. They are treated as sources of money, as something to be manipulated."[20]

Even at this early stage of the grief reaction, feelings of guilt begin to emerge, but rarely is it referred to or even recognized. When the undertaker (sometimes unknowingly) insinuates by word or implication that greater financial investment indicates greater love for the dead, the family will frequently opt for a more expensive ritual.

I do not propose to go into any depth about the funeral. However, one of the most common questions I am asked when I speak to ministers about grief is, "How do you handle the funeral when someone has committed suicide?" The following paragraphs will include several suggestions as to how the funeral of a suicide can be conducted.[21]

Two criteria can be applied in judging the value of the funeral. First, it must portray Christian meaning (about life, death, life after death, community, resurrection, etc.) to the survivors; and secondly, it must aid rather than hinder the grief process of the mourners.

The following are some valid functions of the funeral.

1. The funeral service is an acting-out of feelings which are too difficult to be talked about so soon after the death. Lawrence Abt points out that experiences like the loss of a loved one are of such high emotional content that they are often beyond the capacity of words to express, and accepted patterns of group behavior help to vent these feelings somewhat and prevent their denial.[22] In this respect funeral customs the world over serve to help people vent powerful feelings which need to be expressed for their own good. As Paul Irion states:

> . . . every group in every culture has found it necessary to perform certain rituals at the time of the death of its members. Why? for one simple reason: They do it for themselves. Because they die a little when anyone else dies, they need to verify the dignity and importance of their living and to help guarantee the practices that will protect them from indignity in death when they are helpless and dependent.[23]

The ritual is an important part of a series of experiences which the bereaved must face. It can aid in giving the bereaved the capacity to work through his grief so that he can come out of the situation emotionally sound.[24]

2. A second valuable function of the funeral is to help us affirm the basic assumptions about life which are shattered by the death of one so close. Any crisis, especially death, raises basic questions of purpose and meaning in life. Bowman says:

> The ceremony is . . . a highlighted opportunity in the period following the death for each participant to call on himself to make severe

judgments on his life's loyalties and work, and to make his own "rejoinder to the experiences of life."[25]

3. Another value of the funeral is that it can emphasize the reality of the severed relationship between the living and the dead. Paul Irion states:

> The funeral underscores the reality of the bereavement situation as it offers realistic interpretation of what has taken place . . . the mourner is joined by others in the group who are experiencing something of the same loss. The separation from the body of the deceased by burial or cremation further affirms that the relationship as it has been known has really been broken.[26]

4. The aspect of community, the solace of friends who gather to share the family's grief, is another value of the funeral. Historically, the distinction between the family's grief and that of friends and neighbors was not as sharp as it is today. The family was a cohesive group, but not as distinct from the rest of the community as it is now, and death was a major deprivation for the whole community. The community, the group of concerned friends, the church, can fulfill a very important function in aiding the bereaved. Jackson comments: "The funeral then is a form of group protection, in the face of individual death, to affirm the values of life and the community and direct future living toward these values."[27] Similarly, Irion states:

> The funeral itself is only part, sometimes even a small part, in the whole psychological process of meeting bereavement. Yet, because of its public nature, it is an extremely important part. It represents the responses of the community or of the church to the emotional experiences of the mourners.[28]

5. A final value of the funeral, already alluded to, is that it provides the comfort and stability of religion. In this regard, writes Irion:

> The funeral bears witness to the Christian hope for new life beyond death, to the sustaining love of God even amid suffering, and to the strength which God provides for the facing and accepting of reality. This witness is made not only verbally but in the activity of the Christian community, the church, ministering to the bereaved.[29]

One of the basic functions of Christianity is to give meaning to both life and death. The funeral ritual is a reaffirmation of faith in Christ and in life's meaning, as well as in the meaning of death. I would like to once more quote Paul Irion, who has helped me see the value of the funeral:

> The Christian understanding of life and death and the affirmation of the hope for the resurrection become the basis of the coping function. The church, the Christian community, becomes the supportive group which shares the mourner's sorrow and provides him with the ritual in which he is able to find the meanings through which life and death and all that they entail are understood. The relationship to God and to other members of the Christian community provides the acceptance which frees the mourner to confront the reality of his crisis and to express honestly his feelings toward it.[30]

On the basis of these values I believe there should be changes in present funeral practices which will make them better conveyors of Christian meaning and will aid in the grieving process. The following is a list of five changes which it is hoped will lead to a greater achievement of these values.

1. The needless high cost of funerals creates a burden on many families. Several of the bereaved in the research felt the funeral was helpful but still were shocked at the high cost. One suicide survivor described her experience: "We went through all of the financial end. . . . They were so busy smiling and looking pasty-faced and getting out books for the guests, and oh, really, it was just awful. . . . It was the most terrifying experience—absolutely terrifying. That was worse than the death. . . . It was expensive, and it was macabre, and it was horrible."

I believe the control of funeral practices must go back to social professionals. The extravagance will continue to run away from us until specialists (whether ministers, lawyers, members of memorial societies, or social workers) help families to prepare for funerals before death comes—or, if preparations are not made, aid in giving information about the type of funeral the family wants and names of mortuaries that will perform these services at a reasonable cost.

2. There needs to be a reevaluation of such practices as open caskets, embalming, viewing, etc. For example, I believe there is no

place for the open casket during a funeral service; if the family insists, it can be open before the service. Closing the casket symbolically marks the beginning of the separation, the finality of death, and the changed relationship. People also need to realize that embalming is not necessary. A 1959 funeral industry advertisement claimed: ". . . the embalming of a family's loved one . . . is a service of true reverence . . . the very essence of refined funeral practice."[31] In contrast, Bowman feels the practice of embalming—seeking the long-term preservation of the body—tends to displace and cancel out the far more important work of affirming the finality of death.[32] I believe he is correct in this judgment. Prompt burial or cremation can be substituted for embalming. In any case, funerals must heighten the fact that there has indeed been a death—not to "bang the bereaved over the head" with the fact, but to emphasize it clearly in the funeral or memorial service. Euphemisms such as "slumber," "eternal rest," "passed away," or "is not with us," do not reinforce the reality of death. Nor do slumber rooms, flowers, sweet words, or the restoration of the face. Some funeral directors maintain that the last look at the restored face (the "memory picture" achieved by the use of, among other things, waxes, dyes, cotton padding, plaster of paris, rivets, and chicken wire) is an image to be remembered for all of life and is an asset to what they call grief therapy. Psychologists, however, have testified that the lasting image usually does not originate in the "last look," but rather in experiences with the deceased while he was still alive.[33]

Viewing is another American funeral custom which is of questionable value. Presenting the corpse to friends requires hundreds of dollars' worth of restoration, garments and flowers, and a "respectable" coffin which usually comprises the bulk of funeral costs. Lamm and Eskreis, one a rabbi and the other a psychiatrist, point out in their article that "viewing" serves no positive psychological purpose and may even be harmful. To quote them:

> . . . we believe that, while viewing may seem desirable superficially, deeper consideration will show it to be devoid of real meaning and in fact detrimental in terms of both religion and mental health. Religiously, it expresses disregard for the rights of the dead and a perversion of the religious significance of life and death. Psychologically, it may serve to short-circuit the slow therapy of nature's awareness of death.[34]

I am not ready to state unequivocally that viewing should be abolished, but its value should be very seriously questioned.

Immediate cremation is a very live option for Protestants. Unfortunately it is frowned upon by the funeral industry—indeed in many states the laws forbid a body being cremated without a casket. Ministers and memorial societies need to use their power to change some of these plainly ridiculous laws.[35]

3. Funerals should become a more integral part of the church's ministry. It is an important opportunity for the church to witness to its faith in the resurrection, therefore it is good to hold a funeral in the church rather than in a funeral parlor, under most circumstances. Irion believes that, although the community can gather elsewhere, the church is ". . . a given place where its existence comes into focus most clearly."[36] The whole Christian community mourns, not just a few friends who visit the funeral parlor. Greater support is felt when the Christian community can gather with the family and share in the sorrow. The time of the funeral has some bearing as well. Obligations to work and school make attendance at the customary morning or early afternoon service difficult for all but the intimately involved. Some ministers have successfully experimented with late afternoon or early evening funerals. Wider acceptance of the memorial service, held without the presence of the body, will present few problems since it can easily be scheduled when nearly everyone can attend.

4. Another change I would like to see would be the wholehearted acceptance of a nonreligious funeral by nonreligious people—what has been called a "humanistic" funeral. This is a funeral which is performed in a dignified way not by a minister but by friends of the deceased who do not want to make a sham of the funeral by bringing in religious symbols and language which they do not believe. The purpose would not be to create boundaries between religious and nonreligious people, but rather to create the possibility of more meaningful funerals for both groups. I believe the adoption of the nonreligious humanistic funeral would eliminate some of the superficial quasi-religious practices in funerals for those who find no meaning in them. It would also allow deeply religious individuals to create funerals which would express their faith as well as comfort them in their grief.

5. Greater emphasis on the legitimacy of grieving should be incorporated into the funeral service. The minister can do this in his brief meditation, or it can be included in the liturgy of the funeral or memorial service. An excellent example of this is the order of burial of the Mar Thoma Church of South India:

> It is meet and right for everyone to be sorry for one's own departed: since death is real parting from life here, it is just and proper to weep.

Another way that grieving can be encouraged, and I have found this helpful in my own experience, is to stop for a moment before the benediction or at some other appropriate place in the service and suggest to those gathered that it is acceptable and good to openly mourn this personal loss, and that you, the minister, also grieve. At a memorial service I attended recently, the minister paused briefly before the benediction and said something to this effect: "I have known Robert for only a short time, yet in the few months that we knew each other I came to really like and appreciate him. I too, along with the rest of you, grieve his death this afternoon. It is right in God's eyes and in the church's that you should feel sad and openly cry and grieve his death." These few words helped to relieve the pent-up feelings of several individuals at the service. It is also valuable to develop a relationship with the close survivors *before* the funeral service so that they will trust you enough to express their feelings openly.

I have listed five values of the funeral, and some suggestions for changes. It should be noted that this has not been an attempt to lash out at funeral directors, who obviously provide a much-needed service to the bereaved. Some survivors found the funeral and the funeral director very beneficial in their time of grief. However, if the funeral is not generally helpful to people in their grief work, and it did not appear to be for many in the research, then the value received for its high cost must be radically reconsidered. I believe the financial burden that present funeral practices place on some families outweighs any advantages they might bring, and other more generally helpful forms of "grief therapy" need to be developed. Lowering the cost and making the service more meaningful would be very helpful to those who are initiating a long period of grief.

Dealing with the Aspects of Suicide and Suicide Ideation

A completed suicide presents some unique considerations for the minister, as does the problem of suicide ideation and behavior among the bereaved. In the case of a suicidal death, the amount of openness concerning the cause of death is a prime issue. How you as a minister should handle the funeral service of a person who has committed suicide will depend to some extent upon the situation. Below are listed four common situations with suggestions for handling them.

1. When the cause of death has not yet been determined at the time of the funeral (some people may suspect suicide, but no one *knows*), it is best to handle the funeral as if you were officiating at the service of one who died suddenly of, perhaps, a heart attack. Questions about the means of death are not appropriate at this time. If the coroner should rule it a suicide later on, then the minister can deal with the added burden at that time.

2. Often only a close family member, such as the widow, knows it was a suicide. The cause is covered up ("accident" or "heart attack"), probably with the cooperation of the physician. If you have been told the *real* cause of death, the way you choose to handle this situation must be decided contextually. Openness is very important, and I think the healthiest thing the survivor can do is to make a clean breast of it, to let friends and relatives know the truth. This is much easier than carrying around a terrible secret. However, this may be idealistic in some situations and a second choice is to let the survivor share the secret with you, and all his feelings about it. This will require several counseling sessions during the grief period and the survivor could develop a dependency upon the counselor, but, it may be the best that can be hoped for in such a situation.

3. When the close family and a few friends know it was a suicide but others in the community do not, the minister should again urge the survivors to be honest with the fact that it was a suicide. (In all probability most people will know within the next few weeks anyway—such gossip spreads very quickly.) If they agree, then I believe the suicide should be mentioned somewhere within the funeral service—not to make an issue of it but to deal with the feelings that the survivors have about it.

4. The situation in which everybody knows it was a suicide is generally easiest to handle. However, it will still be important to check out the feelings of the close survivors about mentioning the suicide in the service. Then it should be dealt with openly as suggested in the previous paragraph.

In all of these cases, and in other pastoral care situations as well as the funeral, I think a good rule of thumb is that the more you are able to foster openness with the fact of suicide, the better the chances are for an adaptive grief period. Having to keep the secret that it was a suicide, never knowing what others are thinking, is a burden which makes for a more difficult grief period. It hinders communication with family, friends, and relatives, and also makes it hard for those who suspect or know about the suicide but are not supposed to know, to help the bereaved. If the survivors are open about the suicide, the people close to them will be freer to care for them during their grief.

I am fully aware that convincing the spouse to face up to the suicide is difficult. Some of the individuals in the study told me that their mate's death was *not* a suicide, even though I had read their spouses' suicide notes in the coroner's files. How willing the survivors are to go along with the minister's suggestion to be open about the death will depend to a great degree upon their feeling of trust in him.

Openness or lack of openness concerning the suicide is related to the stigma attached to suicide. Most close survivors feel suicide is a blot upon their family, when actually a few people may criticize them for what they must have done to "drive him to it," but most of their friends are concerned and do not blame them extensively. It is interesting, as pointed out in the last chapter, that the survivors appear to feel more blame leveled at them than appears really to exist. I believe this is a consequence of their failing to deal honestly with the suicide among their acquaintances. As an example, one suicide survivor, whose wife was dying of cancer when she took her own life, said, ". . . a neighbor bugged me about that. And she doesn't know, I didn't tell her. Her house is from here to the door from our house, and to see my wife get in a cab in the driveway, the neighbor says can I help you and she says, no, thank you very much for everything . . . so probably that stirred her curiosity. When people asked me how she died, in the hospital, I say yeah, in the hospital, or something like that. I felt funny about telling a lie, and yet I wanted to skirt this deal."

Another suicide survivor took the opposite approach: she is completely open with the suicide. She says she has felt much comfort in the fact that she isn't hiding anything, though it was difficult at first. To quote her: "I'd tell anybody that asks me. You know, when they hear I'm a widow they say, oh, did your husband have an accident and I say no, he committed suicide. If I lied to them I'd be lying to myself. . . . It's lying because if I said yes, he had an accident, and then they get to know you later and they heard that he committed suicide, they want to know, gee, I wonder why she's hiding it, you know."

The minister also faces special problems when he is dealing with a suicide survivor who exhibits suicide ideation and behavior himself (and indeed a non-suicide survivor as well if he appears suicidal). In this situation he should not get bogged down by dealing with the individual's guilt. The reason for this is that the guilt felt by the individual with suicide ideation is not significantly different from the guilt in the person who has no thoughts of committing suicide, therefore guilt is not a major contributing factor to the suicide ideation. In such a crisis situation it is more important to focus on the person's emotional acceptance of the loss and his involvement with other individuals. The guilt can be handled later, when the crisis is past. The counselor also needs to deal with his religious beliefs—helping him to develop meaning in life, to express it in religious or quasi-religious beliefs, and to live by those beliefs. A person who has religious beliefs and who has developed some meaning in life is to a certain extent immunized from becoming suicidal; individuals who exhibit suicide ideation and behavior are generally less religious than those who do not.

Here again the pastoral counselor, with his unique training in theology, is well equipped to deal with the total character of the suicide situation. It is his job to deal with questions of meaning and faith. Frequently the nontheologically trained counselor will pass over the religious aspects of suicide and thus miss one important resource which he could utilize in helping to mobilize the coping abilities of the survivor. Jackson puts it this way:

> The pastor is not only a counselor with psychological understanding and a concern for the welfare of his parishioners' souls, but he

is also the custodian of a philosophy of life and a concept of the universe that can replace despair with hope, fearfulness with faith, and guilt with feelings of forgiveness.[37]

Suicide ideation and activity in survivors appears to be one of the best indicators of an unadaptive grief reaction. Those who contemplate or attempt suicide during their grief are generally having difficulty adapting in a healthy way to the loss.

The Months following the Crisis Period

Several weeks after the funeral is over and the crisis is past, most of the deceased's acquaintances have stopped talking about him and have gone back to "business as usual." The close survivor has also gone back to work or school, and in many ways things look the same as before. But the suicide survivor has moved into a difficult period because he seems to be suffering alone. Nobody talks about the deceased anymore. Friends stop dropping by. There are no more casseroles and cakes brought to the house. The spouse is left with all the unfinished business of the deceased, plus the double responsibility of being both mother and father to the children.

The main dynamics of grief in the months following the crisis period are depression, guilt, anger, and preoccupation with the loss. The survivor is engaged in a continual struggle to adapt to the new reality of being without his spouse.

One of the struggles during this time is with depression, one of the biggest factors for the first six months (especially the first three months) after the death. This depression is associated with feelings of hostility, guilt, and sometimes suicidal thoughts.

Bouts with depression are centered on feelings of helplessness, hopelessness, and hostility. The worst thing a counselor can do is to listen passively to these feelings. If the survivor is not stimulated to express his hostility in anger and seek new structure and meaning in his life, he will only feel worse. He will feel more helpless because, although he related his feelings and may have felt a little better at first, nothing has changed and he feels even more depressed as a result. I shall suggest several ways in which an individual may deal with his bouts with depression. They are by no means exhaustive but will give an idea of what the bereaved needs.

1. Although survivors frequently experience a loss of friends, especially when their mate committed suicide, they usually have a few close friends whom they can talk to, be with, do things with. The minister can be one of these people who care for the bereaved, not necessarily to counsel them, but just being concerned and ready to be with the bereaved or to talk when they want to. Schnitzer has suggested that the "friends may have nothing to say, but their very presence with the bereaved when he feels that the world is empty and void, has its remedial effects."[38] This is traditionally the role that clergymen have played—maintaining personal contact with the survivors during a grief—and it is sometimes sufficient. At other times the minister will have to intervene more directly.

2. The second help is for the survivor to keep active. This serves to minimize long periods of sitting alone and wallowing in self-pity; it also aids in counteracting the individual's feeling of helplessness. Several suicide spouses expressed surprise that "I actually could do things again." It is not particularly easy. One woman, describing going back to work after the death, said, "The first two days I made more mistakes than I've made in six years at the factory . . . I cried at the least little thing, anybody looked at me crooked, or anybody said anything . . . I think it's responsibility that keeps you together. I mean if you don't have anything then you might be able to sit there and fall apart." She experienced both the difficulty and the satisfaction of being able to do something again. I asked another woman, who was forced by a friend and personal circumstances to take care of many tasks right after the funeral, if it was valuable: "Yes, it was better that I was forced into doing all the businesslike things. But because I stood straight they expected more of me, and they didn't know what was going on inside." Her answer shows both the value and the danger of being active. She felt more ego strength, but at the same time people thought she was adapting to her grief better than she actually was, and they expected more of her.

Regular employment is a way of keeping active. Of the individuals who had worked since the death (both suicide and non-suicide), 88% received a great deal of satisfaction out of their work. Work is not only a place to be active and experience satisfaction in accomplishment, but also a place to be with other people during the lonely months after the death. Some writers on grief, however, warn the bereaved against spending too *much* time working or being active, for fear they will avoid dealing with their grief. This is a real danger, especially for individuals who use their hyperactivity to escape their feelings. In the research for this book the bereaved were discovered to be working more than they had before the death, and I had considerable difficulty in reaching a number of them because of their long hours. Keeping active can be as much an escape from dealing with the loss as sitting alone is an escape from responsible activity.

The idea behind the suggestion to have the bereaved keep active to avoid becoming immobilized by grief is seen in O. Hobart Mowrer's statement, "It is easier to act your way into a new way of *feeling* than to feel your way into a new way of acting."[39] This is important because after a death feelings of helplessness and hopelessness are common. The fact that the bereaved *can* go to work again, *can* meet new friends, *can* take over some of the responsibilities of the deceased, and so forth, builds up the self-confidence which is often at a low ebb after the death, and gives him renewed hope that he will be able to create a new life for himself without the deceased. The immobilized individual who does not resume his normal activities can easily develop a seriously unadaptive grief.

3. A third help for the survivor is *involvement in organizations*. The group can be a chess club, a singles club, a choir, a church group, and the like. This offers not only activity but also another opportunity to be with people. One such group is Parents Without Partners (PWP).[40] Probably the chief value of the group is that the members all have basically the same problem. This gives confidence to the bereaved and divorced persons. PWP offers these people new friends, helpful discussions, and lectures on various aspects of their new life. A man who was involved in PWP said, "Talking with people maybe sometimes I'd feel that my position was unique, a widower with a daughter, and then you'd see a widow or widower with three, four, five kids, and I'd think, gee, it isn't so bad after all; they have problems too. And as I became more involved in PWP and became more active in it, I did more. . . . I think the thing that helped me more than anything else to get back to a normal type of relationship and decide or want to remarry, was my concern for others and wanting to help them, because that helping helped me." A woman said, "From my own experience I found that I recovered from the shock of death through my own efforts and joining Parents Without Partners. This group was a very big help as a crutch.

When I found that I no longer needed a crutch I withdrew from the organization and began life anew, with few regrets, good memories, and a determination to live and enjoy."

4. A fourth help is the process of *creating new friends*. Engel, a specialist in psychosomatic medicine, has said, "If grief is a reaction to an object loss, then the maintenance and replacement of objects [persons in relation] must be considered an important factor in the healing process."[41] For a number of spouses in the research, creating new friends led to remarriage. These individuals were adapting to their grief better than those who hadn't remarried. There is no easy answer to how long a person should wait before remarrying; I personally feel an individual should usually wait six months, after which the intensity of a normal grief subsides. Since grieving continues for many years after the death of one so close, waiting to remarry until the grief is past is asking for three to five years or more alone, and this is usually unnecessary. If you find in pre-marriage counseling that the widowed spouse still has considerable difficulty adapting to the loss, it is advisable that they wait several more months. If the individual is adapting well to the grief three to six sessions of pre-marriage counseling is generally helpful in opening up the widowed individual's feeling about the deceased and in helping the couple to create a new life together.

Developing new friends is helpful in freeing a person from preoccupation with the loss. It is an opportunity to redirect the love and need-satisfaction from the deceased to new persons.

5. The fifth help during this period is for the pastoral counselor to *bring into the open any hostility* that is festering in the depressed survivor. This can be done in many ways, such as chair dialoguing (to be discussed in the next section). Another way, which I have found helpful, is to have the individual hit a pillow or cushion; I may suggest they close their eyes and imagine the deceased's face on the pillow, then hit it. You frequently have to be quite directive to convince the person to do it. After really belting the pillow until he is exhausted, he will often end up hugging it, symbolizing the ambivalence of love and anger for the deceased. Another effective method is to purposely berate the spouse until he becomes very angry at the counselor. (It is important that you are able to handle anger fairly well or this should not be attempted.) This anger is then redirected to the deceased spouse.

6. A final help during this period is to help the individual re-discover meaning in life. Several of the above suggestions will aid in this task. As an individual becomes active in groups and learns to give of himself in love to new individuals, he is already redis-covering hope.

Meaning is developed by the bereaved on two levels. First, on the *relational and emotional level,* the freeing from preoccupation with the loss and the reinvesting of love in new relationships with others helps the bereaved to achieve meaning.[42] On this level meaning is realized in three ways, according to Frankl. The first is by doing a deed, by accomplishing or achieving something, e.g., helping some-one else who is in need.[43] The second way is by experiencing some-thing—such as a work of nature, the caring of another individual, the love of God. When the bereaved individual experiences the love of his minister and fellow church members he can thus experience the love of God and in so doing rediscover meaning in his life. The third way of discovering meaning on the relational and emotional level is in suffering. The grief period is certainly an experience of suffering and can therefore be a fruitful period for discovering meaning. The challenge for the individual is not only to see the grief period as a time of unhappiness, but to find meaning and hope in his suffering. To quote Frankl:

> Whenever one is confronted with an inescapable, unavoidable situation, whenever one has to face a fate that cannot be changed, e.g., an incurable disease, such as inoperable cancer, just then is one given a last chance to actualize the highest value, to fullfill the deepest meaning, the meaning of suffering. For what matters above all is the attitude we take toward suffering, the attitude in which we take our suffering upon ourselves.[44]

The second level on which meaning develops is the *conceptual level.* Putting the experiences of suffering, of love, of doing some-thing for someone else, into meaningful symbols, helps to reinforce these experiences in a positive way. Meaning in life includes both experiences and beliefs (ethics, conceptualization of life-style, etc.). Switzer says:

> We cannot really exist as fully human without a sense of coherence, purpose, value, and an understanding of our own roles in the larger life about us. When all of this is challenged by the death of some-

one who has been involved in the production of meaning in our lives, there is the sense of threat, the rise of anxiety which we call grief.[45]

If an individual sees his bereavement as a totally meaningless and useless experience, he will find it very difficult to construct a new life without the deceased. But the bereaved who is willing to search for meaning in his suffering as well as in the caring of others for him, which he can experience as the love of God, has a considerably better chance to adapt well to his grief and his new way of living.

Guilt

If one aspect were to be singled out as the outstanding factor that distinguishes suicide spouses from non-suicide spouses, it would probably be guilt. The church and the pastoral counseling minister have something very important to say concerning the issue of guilt. LeRoy Aden, in "Pastoral Counseling as Christian Perspective," maintains that what makes the pastoral counselor unique in his identity is that he works from "a Christian perspective which seeks to help or to heal by attending to the life situation of the troubled person."[46] Aden maintains that this Christian perspective may not be very evident from a cursory examination of his counseling techniques, but is seen at crucial points in his counseling. Aden identifies three marks of the Christian perspective: (1) the problem of finitude; (2) the problem of alienation; and (3) the problem of guilt. He indicates that the problem of finitude is a grappling with the limitations of life; the problem of alienation with life's meaning; and the problem of guilt with fulfillment.[47]

The minister needs to help the suicide survivor especially to deal with guilt. It can appear as a sense of shame or failure, or as hopelessness and helplessness; it can be experienced as unworthiness or as an attitude of rebellion and disobedience. The Christian answer (using Tillich's method of correlation) to guilt is *forgiveness*, to quote Aden:

> . . . because it assures men of being "accepted in spite of his being unacceptable." Pastoral counseling, therefore, in attending to the client's struggle with guilt, seeks to help him move toward . . . the acceptance of forgiveness.[48]

How can the pastoral counselor aid in the achievement of forgiveness? A number of methods are valuable in dealing with guilt. These methods can also be of help in working with other phases of the grief reaction, but guilt is probably the most important aspect of the suicide grief that the minister will deal with.

Just talking about the guilt—sharing and confessing it with another person—is helpful, even more so when the individual can share his guilt feelings in a group and still feel accepted by the members. For the minister this indicates (1) the necessity of acceptance, and (2) the value of confession. Let us look at both of these aspects more fully. It is crucial in all counseling of guilt that the client feel he is accepted at a deep level, even though the counselor (and probably the client) may not like what he has done. The counselor's acceptance of the client in turn helps him to accept himself more fully. Confession is an established Christian practice. Although private confession has fallen into disuse in many Protestant churches, acknowledgment of guilt is a crucial aspect of pastoral counseling.

The traditional process of (1) confession or acknowledgment of one's guilt, (2) acceptance of forgiveness and absolution, (3) restitution for wrongs done when possible, and (4) amendment of life, is still very viable.

The self-disclosure of the secrets that make one feel guilty is the first step in this process. Jackson comments, "When this activity is directed toward a creative newness of life, the tendency is to move away from morbid preoccupation with the past toward a healthy participation in the present and future."[49] One problem the minister needs to be aware of, which psychiatrists and psychologists like Fromm, Parlour, Mowrer, and others point out, is that the individual may plead guilty to lesser crimes and not speak of his real guilt feelings. The alert minister can penetrate the facade and get at the real feelings of guilt—perhaps that the person thinks he caused the death, or that he feels he is a failure as a person because of his spouse's suicide, etc. The pastoral counselor helps the person confess what he is really guilty of. Stein puts it this way:

> The most important task of the pastoral counselor . . . is to help the counselee shift his concern from guilt feelings to what he genuinely *is* guilty of and to help the person explore and find ways of making value decisions about his life and acting on these. This means accepting responsibility for his life and authentically affirming

it, moving toward self-actualization. This does not deny guilt, it accepts its reality, and redirects it toward channels that produce more lasting self-esteem and minimize not only the tendency toward, but the necessity for, self-punishment.[50]

The second step in this process of dealing with guilt—acceptance of forgiveness and absolution—is difficult for any but a religiously oriented counselor to bring about in cases of guilt focused on what a person did to the deceased or to God. Jackson states, "When the person who could forgive is no longer present the effectiveness of an oversoul capable of forgiving is a source of release and comfort."[51] The minister has the advantage of being able to pray with him for forgiveness of legitimate wrongs and give absolution. Prayer and absolution should not, however, become shortcuts to the working through of guilt.

Protestants, in their zeal to affirm salvation *sola gratia,* have tended to deemphasize the importance of restitution and amendment of life. It is therapeutically valuable for the guilt-laden individual to make restitution for the wrongs he has done. The form which this restitution takes is open to the individual. Stein states, "It is possible for a person to eliminate a guilt feeling by going through an act of restitution—paying a price."[52] The minister must be careful that the individual does not construe his worth and acceptance as being based upon doing acts of restitution. He needs to be aware that as a human being he is already forgiven by God. Restitution is not a way of bribing God or others into accepting him.

Amendment of life is the final aspect in the process of dealing with guilt. The individual, after evaluating his relationship with the deceased, makes a commitment to act differently, and then acts upon his commitment. This change of behavior can be very valuable from the standpoint of preventative pastoral counseling in aiding the suicide survivor is not repeating many of his mistakes in subsequent interpersonal relationships.

The process of confession, acceptance of forgiveness and absolution, restitution, and amendment of life does not have to occur as a liturgical ritual; frequently it will happen without the client's explicit awareness of what has happened. However, the basic process is a model of dealing with guilt in the bereaved.

There are several different methods in which guilt that seems blocked can be freed, so that the person can move toward forgiveness. The following paragraphs will suggest a few of these techniques.

Dorpat has indicated in conversations with the author that the guilt of suicide survivors frequently has a grandiose and irrational element to it—"If I had just come home from work earlier, I would have been able to save her," or "If I had just not argued with her then she would not have killed herself." The method Dorpat has found most helpful in such cases is "gently debunking" these grandiose assumptions and confronting the client with the reality that he could probably not have stopped the suicide.

A third technique of dealing with the guilt of a suicide survivor (also useful with other problems of the grief reaction) is *chair dialoguing*. One way of doing this is to place an empty chair in front of the client and say, "This (pointing to the chair) is the feeling of guilt you have been talking about. I want you to give it a voice and let it speak to you." Another way, which seems more valuable to the author, is to tell the client that his deceased spouse is in the empty chair and ask the client to talk to him. In both cases the client moves back and forth between the two chairs and speaks for both sides. If he gets bogged down in the dialogue the counselor can step into one of the parts and play it for a while, then step out when the dialogue is moving again. Chair dialoguing may be one of the best techniques for helping individuals with their grief.[53]

Another method which, like chair dialoguing, is helpful for other aspects of the grief reaction as well, is reviewing the client's life with the deceased, starting early in the marriage and moving slowly forward to the actual death and the events shortly thereafter. This technique can be used in several ways. First, the minister can simply ask the client to review his life with the deceased and repeat the review several times until his anxiety and guilt about the death have decreased. A second method of review uses desensitization. The counselor and client compile a list of events which preceded the death in ascending order of anxiety and guilt, and proceed as with any other problem dealt with by desensitization.[54] A third method of review combines the above two methods. The client sits in a relaxed position and closes his eyes, then the counselor reviews with him his relationship with the deceased, and the client visualizes the events and describes and evaluates them with the counselor. From time to time the counselor asks him to open his eyes and discuss what he has visualized. The process continues until the client visualizes the actual death scene and the deceased, and can talk about it without too great a level of anxiety.

The above are a few valuable methods of intervention with a survivor's guilt. Jackson states, "It is in this area that the alert pastoral counselor can assist in working through the guilt and freeing the personality from the deep and disturbing feelings that might cripple it for an indefinite period."[55]

The Unadaptive Grief

There are a number of warning signs which may clue the counselor that an unadaptive grief is forming. In developing the following list I have drawn upon the present research as well as upon the works of Lindemann and others. The warning signs are:

1. A serious medical disease, especially of psychosomatic nature such as spastic or ulcerative colitis, asthma, rheumatoid arthritis, etc.

2. Gross over- or underactivity. Associated with overactivity is a sense of well-being as if the loss had not occurred. Associated with underactivity is apathy towards life, retardation or lack of speech, and minimal interpersonal contacts.

3. Getting "stuck" in the shock state, acting mechanically like a robot rather than living and feeling life.

4. Any psychotic behavior.

5. An agitated depression.

6. Constantly acting out the loss behaviorally, such as by failing repeatedly in business or marriage, etc.

7. Unresolved anger which even when expressed brings no release.

8. Pretending that the deceased is still living.

9. Suicidal ideation or activity.

10. A marked unadaptive alteration in the individual's style of interpersonal relationships with family, relatives, and friends.

11. Loss of pattern of social relationships; not readapting to society.

12. Broken-down family relationships.

13. Remarriage to a chronically ill, physically handicapped, or suicidal individual.

14. Severe guilt which causes the person to constantly blame and punish himself physically or mentally.

When any of these signs occur in the grief reaction of the suicide survivor, and it appears that there may be other severe disturbances, the minister must intervene and attempt to get the survivor into counseling. If he feels he is not able to counsel the individual effectively, the minister should seek consultation or transfer the person to a skilled and highly trained pastoral counselor or psychotherapist. If the individual is suffering seriously from one or more of the warning signs—especially if he is exhibiting any behavior which appears psychotic—the minister should immediately seek psychiatric help. The individual may need to be hospitalized.

Summary

Understanding the dynamics of the suicide grief reaction is only half of the process towards aiding a person in his grief. The minister or counselor must also know methods of counseling the bereaved. Each survivor is a completely unique individual with a unique response to his loss; yet some generalized techniques can be valuable in helping him, if used skillfully by the minister.

Every individual who counsels the bereaved needs to come to terms with his own feelings about death and suicide, lest they hinder his work. When this is accomplished a relationship of empathy—wherein the minister senses deeply the feelings of the bereaved and yet realizes that there is a distinction between the bereaved and himself—has the opportunity to occur.

An extremely important part of the pastor's task to the suicide survivor is his ministry during the period of crisis, including the funeral. These first days and weeks after the death are the time when an individual's style of adapting to a grief is formed. The "ABC" method of crisis intervention counseling (A: Achieve contact, B: Boil down and focus the problem, C: Challenge the person to cope) readily lends itself to caring for suicide survivors. The fact that it is a suicide death is best dealt with as openly as the survivor can possibly handle. This openness can allay or prevent later problems.

The major problem of guilt after a suicide must be dealt with if the survivors are to adapt well to their grief. Sharing one's feelings of guilt, accepting God's forgiveness, and changing or amending one's life, are valuable in constructively handling the guilt.

Finally, if the minister senses that an individual is suffering from any of the warning signs of a seriously unadaptive grief, he should immediately seek consultation or refer the person to a mental health professional.

NOTES

1. Dietrich Bonhoeffer, *Ethics* (New York: Macmillan, 1955), p. 126.

2. Daniel Day Williams, *The Minister and the Care of Souls* (New York: Harper & Brothers, 1961), p. 60.

3. For further reading concerning the pastor-parishioner relationship I would suggest the first few chapters of Howard Clinebell's *Basic Types of Pastoral Counseling* (New York: Abingdon Press, 1966); also Sidney M. Jourard's book, *The Transparent Self* (Princeton, N.J.: D. Van Nostrand Co., 1964); Carl R. Rogers's *Client-Centered Therapy* (Boston: Houghton Mifflin, 1951) and in his book *Counseling and Psychotherapy* (Boston: Houghton Mifflin, 1942), the portion dealing with "The Creation of a Counseling Relationship," pp. 85–114; also the first chapter of William Glasser's book, *Reality Therapy* (New York: Harper and Row, 1965).

4. C. Charles Bachmann, *Ministering to the Grief Sufferer* (Philadelphia: Fortress Press, 1967), p. 26.

5. See definition of crisis in Glossary.

6. Julian R. Taplin, "Crisis Theory: Critique and Reformulation," *Community Mental Health Journal* VII:1 (1971): 15–16.

7. Wilbur Morley, "Theory of Crisis Intervention," *Pastoral Psychology* XXI:203 (April, 1970): 16.

8. Taplin, "Crisis Theory: Critique and Reformulation," p. 15.

9. Charles Anderson, "Aspects of Pathological Grief and Mourning," *International Journal of Psycho-Analysis* XXX (1949): 48–55.

10. See Glossary for definition of crisis intervention counseling.

11. Warren Jones, "The A-B-C Method of Crisis Management," *Mental Hygiene* LII:1 (January, 1968).

12. Quoted by Howard J. Clinebell, Jr., in a movie, "New Approaches to Crisis Counseling," available through the South Carolina Department of Mental Health.

13. This does not mean that you cannot help the survivor who comes to you for counseling some time after the death, but only that if you *are* with the bereaved at the time of death and he doesn't sense your concern, then it is unlikely that you can help him later.

14. For further discussion of the relationship in crisis intervention counseling, see Shelvey Holland, "Crisis Counseling: A Model for Ministers" (Rel. D. dissertation, School of Theology at Claremont, Claremont, California, 1970), pp. 128–29; and Louis Paul, "Crisis Intervention," *The Clergy and People in Crisis: Proceedings of a Day Institute* (Los Angeles: Los Angeles County Department of Mental Health and Mental Health Development Program, 1965), pp. 18–20.

15. See Chapter 3 for a fuller exploration of these different components of grief.

16. Clinebell, in the movie, "New Approaches to Crisis Counseling."

17. Clinebell, *Basic Types of Pastoral Counseling,* p. 168.

18. See discussion later in this chapter on helping the bereaved to keep active, pp. 89–90.

19. Robert L. Fulton, "The Clergyman and the Funeral Director: A Study in Role Conflict," *Social Forces* XXXIX:4 (May, 1961): 320.

20. Cornell Capa, "Outrage Over the Death Business," *Life* LV:12 (September 20, 1963): 108.

21. I am collecting data on this subject. Readers who are willing to share with me funeral sermons which were effective in meeting the needs of the suicide survivors, or anything else that was helpful, are asked to send them to me in care of the publisher. The book *Brief Funeral Meditations for Unusual Situations* by Charles M. Chakour (New York: Abingdon Press, 1971) contains several sermons for a suicide death as well as for other unusual deaths.

22. Lawrence Abt and S. L. Weisman, eds., *Acting Out* (New York: Grune & Stratton, 1965).

23. Paul E. Irion, *The Funeral: Vestige or Value?* (New York: Abingdon Press, 1966), p. 100.

24. Edgar N. Jackson, *The Christian Funeral* (New York: Channel Press, 1966), pp. 22–23.

25. Leroy Bowman, *The American Funeral* (Washington, D.C.: Public Affairs Press, 1959), p. 142.

26. Irion, *The Funeral: Vestige or Value?* p. 101.

27. Jackson, *The Christian Funeral,* p. 15.

28. Irion, *The Funeral: Vestige or Value?* p. 104.

29. Ibid., p. 10.

30. Ibid., p. 126.

31. Quoted in Bowman, *The American Funeral,* p. 166.

32. Ibid., pp. 167–68.

33. See especially Willard Waller, *The Family, A Dynamic Interpretation* (New York: Cordon Co., 1938), pp. 49 ff.

34. Maurice Lamm and Naftali Eskreis, "Viewing the Remains: A New American Custom," *Journal of Religious and Mental Health* V:2 (April, 1966): 138.

35. Related to this is the requirement for burial vaults, which are sold to 62% of all clients. They are concrete, metal, or fiber glass outer receptacles which encase the casket, for the purpose of greater preservation of the body and grave site. Average retail price is $159.00. See Obert Q. Maisel, "Facts You Should Know About Funerals," *Reader's Digest* (September, 1966): 6.

36. Irion, *The Funeral: Vestige or Value?* p. 188.

37. Edgar Jackson, *Understanding Grief* (New York: Abingdon Press, 1957), p. 160.

38. Jeshaia Schnitzer, "Thoughts on Bereavement and Grief," *Reconstructionist* CXXXI (1955): 12.

39. O. Hobart Mowrer, from *Critical Incidents in Psychotherapy,* ed. S. W. Standel and Raymond J. Corsini (Englewood Cliffs, N.J.: Prentice-Hall, 1959), p. 80.

40. For further information, contact Parents Without Partners International, Inc., International Headquarters, 7910 Woodmont Avenue, Washington, D.C. 20014.

41. G. Engel, "Is Grief a Disease?" *Psychosomatic Medicine* XXIII (1961): 22.

42. David K. Switzer, *Dynamics of Grief* (New York: Abingdon Press, 1970), pp. 203-4.

43. Viktor E. Frankl, *Man's Search for Meaning* (New York: Washington Square Press, Inc., 1963), p. 176.

44. Ibid., p. 178.

45. Switzer, *Dynamics of Grief*, p. 203.

46. LeRoy Aden, "Pastoral Counseling as Christian Perspective," in *The Dialogue Between Theology and Psychology*, ed. Peter Homans (Chicago: University of Chicago Press, 1968), p. 167.

47. Ibid., pp. 173-81.

48. Ibid., p. 181.

49. Jackson, *Understanding Grief*, p. 128.

50. Edward V. Stein, *Guilt: Theory and Therapy* (Philadelphia: Westminster Press, 1968), p. 189.

51. Jackson, *Understanding Grief*, p. 128.

52. Stein, *Guilt: Theory and Therapy*, p. 164.

53. Chair dialoguing is a technique used especially by Gestalt psychotherapists and requires some skill in using it. Frederick S. Perl's book, *Gestalt Therapy Verbatim* (Lafayette, Calif.: Real People Press, 1969) is helpful in illustrating how it is used.

54. The use of desensitization requires considerable clinical skill and is generally used only by a specialist in behavioral therapy. Further information on desensitization can be found in Robert R. Carkhuff's first volume of *Helping and Human Relations* (New York: Holt, Rinehart & Winston, Inc., 1969), pp. 271-90, or in Joseph Wolpe's book *Psychotherapy by Reciprocal Inhibition* (Stanford, Calif.: Stanford University Press, 1958).

55. Jackson, *Understanding Grief*, p. 101.

6. PREVENTATIVE
PASTORAL CARE

In this final chapter I will suggest some ways in which the incidence of destructive suicide grief reactions can be reduced. The conceptual model for preventative pastoral care has been adapted from Gerald Caplan's *Principles of Preventative Psychiatry.*[1]

Three Levels of Preventative Pastoral Care

1. *Primary prevention* is aimed at reducing the incidence of emotional problems and hence unadaptive grief reactions. Its focus is not necessarily on seeking to prevent a specific individual from developing an unadaptive grief reaction, but rather to reduce the risk for every individual who suffers a grief so that the number of individuals who react unadaptively will be reduced. To quote Caplan:

> When a program of primary prevention deals with an individual, he is seen as the representative of a group, and his treatment is determined not only by his own needs, but in relation to the extent of the community problem he represents and the resources available to deal with it.[2]

The concern of primary prevention is not only for what causes people to develop unadaptive grief reactions, but also for why other people have *not,* when living under the same conditions. Such information is used to aid in changing the community so that a smaller number of people will react unadaptively to death.

2. *Secondary prevention* attempts to reduce the duration of a troublesome grief. It aids an individual who is grieving to react in a more "normal" or adaptive way rather than becoming more deeply disturbed. Secondary prevention involves a program aimed at re-

ducing the disability rate of those who are responding unadaptively to a death. This is done through *early diagnosis* and *prompt and effective treatment*. Early diagnosis is the effort to discern the signs of trouble in an individual's grief. It is important because, as in most new patterns of a person's personality structure, the earlier they are discovered and an effective attempt is made to change them, the easier they will be to correct. Behavioral patterns become more fixed with time. Early diagnosis is effective, however, only if it leads to early and effective treatment. This means that there should be no long waiting lists at counseling centers. Treatment should be only for those who are not expected to recover spontaneously.

3. *Tertiary prevention* aims at reducing the extent of impairment in the lives of those who have not adapted well to the death of someone close to them. It involves large-scale rehabilitation of a person's life to aid his quick return to society at as high a level of functioning as possible. It is a community-oriented concept because its main goal is to lower the total number of emotionally plagued individuals and not just to rehabilitate an isolated individual. Caplan describes tertiary prevention as ". . . reducing the rate of residual defect, the lowered capacity to contribute to the occupational and social life of the community which continues after the problem [of suicide in a person] has ended."[3]

Tertiary prevention involves: (1) continuing to care for the bereaved after his therapy is over to enhance his maximum functioning in the community; (2) continuing to check the milieu in which he exists to see if social changes are needed; (3) counteracting the alienation which comes with the stigma of suicide, not only on an individual level but also through primary prevention which aims at education of the community; (4) maintaining communication with one who is in a mental hospital so that the total social network he was involved in outside is kept open and when he leaves the hospital he can take his place at home and at work—one way to aid this is to keep hospitalization at a minimum; (5) utilizing transitional institutions like halfway houses or sheltered workshops where people who have been institutionalized can be reacclimated to the world outside; (6) occupational rehabilitation; and (7) maintaining institutions for the chronically suicidal and psychotic, *only* for those not able to function in normal life.

Suggested Methods of Preventative Pastoral Care

The bulk of this book has focused on secondary and, to a lesser extent, tertiary prevention. In these final pages I shall suggest some ways in which the pastor can attempt to reduce the possibility of unadaptive grief reactions among his parishioners (*primary prevention*). The list of ideas presented below is by no means complete but may give the reader an idea of the possibilities.

1. First is education. Ministers and others in helping professions can be educated about the basic dynamics of grief, and the special problems encountered in very upsetting deaths. Such education should not only focus on the theoretical aspects of grief, but should also involve the minister in reviewing his own past griefs, sensing his own feelings about death, and working out his own theology (or philosophy) of death.

Another need is to train people who frequently come in contact with highly suicidal individuals or survivors of a suicide. Physicians have an excellent opportunity for identification and intervention in suicidal crises, as a large number of suicide victims consult a doctor prior to their act. In *Americans View Their Mental Health* it is reported that 42% of all people who have an emotional problem go to their minister first;[4] thus the minister is also in a key position to intervene in a suicidal crisis as well as in its aftermath. Unfortunately, not all doctors or ministers are doing an adequate job of early detection or rapid treatment of these problems. Doctors, nurses, police, teachers, ministers, social workers, etc., need to be educated both in suicide prevention and in the dynamics and methods of handling grief after a suicide. They have to know what to do and whom to call if they come across someone who is not adapting well to a grief or who appears suicidal. Shneidman and Mandelkorn claim that

> . . . almost everyone who seriously intends suicide leaves clues as to his imminent action. . . . But the suicide decision is usually not impulsive. Most often it is premeditated. . . . It is not impossible, then, to spot a potential suicide if one only knows what to look for.[5]

I believe that the general population also should be educated about grief and the special problems encountered in a suicide death, and have some knowledge of whom to turn to if they sense trouble in a family member or friend. This can be done through Christian education in the congregation. Church school teachers could profit by special training in this area. Also, the pastor or another competent person could teach special limited-time courses at the church for teen-agers and adults dealing with funerals, death, suicide, etc. People of all ages can be educated in problem-solving techniques for dealing with crises. In a crisis situation thinking tends to become poralized, and one who is trained in problem-solving techniques of dealing with crises is generally better able to weather the storm. This can be taught in adult education classes, public school health classes, and in church.

2. Secondly, there is a need to expose popular myths about death and grief. Americans particularly, while on the one hand trying to avoid death completely, on the other hand entertain many naive fantasies about death—many of which may be formed by television and motion pictures. Americans need to be exposed to the reality of death and learn how to come to grips with it.

3. Ministers, lawyers, and memorial societies can help people plan in advance for death. Every married person needs to consider his own death and the death of his spouse, and it is helpful if they together work out funeral and post-funeral arrangements for themselves in advance.

4. Another need, suggested earlier, is a radical reevaluation of the funeral process as a whole. Funeral practices can be developed which would aid the bereaved in their grief. Funeral costs should be lowered so as not to place a hardship upon the survivors. More valuable and need-satisfying methods of grief therapy can be developed —one possibility would be for funeral establishments to hire pastoral counselors who would do follow-up work with each bereaved family over a two-year period following the death. Another possibility was suggested by the results of the intensive interviews: several interviewees indicated that they felt better about the death after talking frankly about it, and for several it was the first time they had ever talked in depth about their loss. Thus it could be that the minister/counselor should consider it part of his task to talk periodically with recent survivors. These talks would serve as primary preventive counseling whereby any blocked aspect of the individual's grief could be dealt with, and they could help to prevent what Lindemann calls "morbid" grief reactions.

It would also be helpful for the coroner's office to hire mental health professionals or for the suicide prevention center to send volunteers immediately to the home of the suicide survivors, to aid them in their special grief. The minister or counselor who does this would continue to visit the survivor periodically over a two-year period or until he has adapted well to his loss.

5. In a family where one member is highly suicidal, the minister can prepare the other members for his possible suicide. Jackson says, "Often irritations can be ventilated and aggressive feelings externalized, so that the death experience does not release all at once the ambivalent feelings that may exist."[6] Sometimes a highly suicidal person will keep his family in tow by threatening to kill himself if they make life hard for him. This makes the others furious but frequently they are afraid to express this anger for fear that he will carry out his threat. This causes an accumulation of pent-up feelings among the members of his family. If he actually does commit suicide, the survivors struggle both with their pent-up anger at the deceased, and with feelings of guilt for being angry and perhaps having "caused" the death.

It is helpful if the minister can work with a family when there is a possibility that a suicide might occur, urging them to express their feelings and offering them a chance to work out these feelings beforehand. This can help in two ways: first, the family already has the minister to go to to talk about their feelings if the death occurs, and secondly, by preparing the survivors the minister can lessen the chance of an unadaptive grief.

6. Preparation for death begins long before a person is born, with the attitudes of his family toward life and death. I believe it is important to help children deal with death at an early age as part of their training. Parents need to know that it is best to be open with their children about death rather than covering it up, such as by saying, "Daddy has gone away on a long trip." Children intuitively sense the duplicity between the words and the feelings transmitted by the surviving parent. To quote Jackson:

> Children, at even an early age, are able more adequately to withstand the stress brought by their limited understanding of death than they are to withstand the mystery and the implied desertion that would be a part of the fabric of falsehood. . . . It is probably reasonable to assume that the earlier a child is introduced to a calm, objective interpretation of death, the sooner he will be able to begin the emotional conditioning that will be his best equipment for

effective mourning when the experience of mature years comes upon him.[7]

This calm, secure attitude in the parent is communicated more through feelings than through words. It is in this way that the child develops his ideas and feelings about death and forms his style of reacting to it at a later time.

7. More groups like Parents Without Partners are needed both within and outside of the church. Those individuals in this study who attended such organizations found them very helpful in their grief. However, people who do not have children under twenty-one years of age are often left out of such groups and they need to be included. It might be valuable for some churches to set up small groups of recently widowed spouses which could focus on their helping each other to accept their loss.

8. Another suggestion concerns meaning in life. Problems of meaning in life occurred with subjects who responded that what gave them meaning in life was their involvement with their spouses or families, to the exclusion of other aspects of life. Grief in such cases involves a substantial loss which can lead to depression and even suicide ideation and activity. If an individual focuses most of his meaning upon his children (as discussed in Chapter 4), he is in for trouble when they leave home. The problems resulting from too narrow a focus of meaning in life points to the need for developing deep interpersonal relationships with individuals beyond the small family group. It is dangerous to invest oneself in only one other person.

In this rapidly changing world, there is a need for individuals to develop beliefs (about God, the world, caring for others, etc.) through which they can conceptualize their experiences and in which they can invest themselves. I am not suggesting that everyone needs a complete set of beliefs and rules which he follows rigidly, but it has been my experience that many of the people who come for counseling live in a world of chaos and are pushed around by the slightest wind that blows. What they seem to need is to begin to discover something they believe in, and develop a life-style in which they can meet the world.

9. Another way the church might help the bereaved is to establish a lay task force group on grief "to surround the bereaved persons with Christian concern," as one Minneapolis church has done.[8]

The purpose of this task force would be for several of its members to establish an ongoing relationship with each bereaved family through frequent visits during the more neglected periods of the grief. Here is an opportunity for laymen to express their Christian concern concretely.

10. Another area of influence in preventative work can be sermons dealing with death, especially appropriate on All Saints' Day or during the Lenten and Christmas seasons. They can be initiators of discussion groups later. If the minister preaches about resurrection, life after death, and hope, but transmits nonverbal feelings of anxiety, fear, and hopelessness, then in all likelihood it is these latter feelings which the listeners will remember and not a calm hope in Christ. If the bereaved remember a warm confident faith being expressed by the minister in his preaching, then they will feel freer to turn to him for guidance when problems occur.

11. A final suggestion in primary prevention is the establishment and utilization of suicide prevention centers. As Maris has asked, "Why does almost every city in the United States over 100,000 population have an organized tuberculosis prevention center, but only a few cities have a suicide prevention center?"[9] Crisis centers or suicide prevention centers need to be established in every city of any size, with a trained staff that can be reached seven days a week and twenty-four hours a day, and which can deal effectively with people who are considering suicide. According to Schneidman:

> Distraught people who phone a crises center . . . consider suicide with great psychological ambivalence. Their wish to die exists simultaneously with a wish to be rescued and survive. We believe that the suicidal crisis has unique features in which life and death frequently hang in the balance. Focused resources are needed for those focused emergencies.[10]

In addition, suicide prevention centers could devote more energy to research in helping the suicide survivor. Their task ought to be broader than just trying to prevent suicide; they need to deal with the aftermath of a completed suicide as well.

All of these suggested methods of preventative pastoral care could help survivors of a suicide to better cope with the stigma, the guilt, the anger, and the feelings of isolation that they sense. It is the hope of the author that some of these methods can be instigated in an effort to ease the pain of such an individual, and perhaps even prevent another suicide.

Summary of the Book

This book has directed itself to two questions about the aftermath of suicide: "Is the grief after a suicide different?" and "How do I as a minister or counselor help the bereaved after someone commits suicide?"

Grief itself, described as the psychological response of the bereaved to the loss of a loved one by death, is characterized by seven major dynamics which are found in both suicide and non-suicide grief reactions: shock, catharsis, depression, guilt, preoccupation with the loss, anger, and acceptance of reality. In comparing the suicide grief with grief following natural or accidental death, a greater amount of guilt was found among survivors of a suicide. Associated with this guilt is more anger directed at the deceased. Also, the suicide survivor senses the stigma of suicide and feels blamed to some extent for the death of his partner. His grief is acted out in more psychosomatic symptoms—physical illness—than the grief of a non-suicide survivor. Also, other investigators have found among suicide survivors a greater tendency to act out their grief by suicide gestures. Appendix B lists the statistical findings related to the differences between the suicide and non-suicide grief.

When someone commits suicide, the minister's first opportunity to help the bereaved is during the crisis period and the funeral, and his intervention at this time can greatly affect the survivor's total response to the death in the months to come. The early weeks of grief are very important in determining how well an individual will adapt to his loss. The great amount of guilt felt by suicide survivors is an area in which the minister can be especially helpful. It was found that the traditional course of confession, with the bereaved revealing his feelings of guilt and experiencing forgiveness and a change of behavior, is still a viable and healing process. The practice of confession is being enriched with insights from psychotherapy so that it need not be a rigid formula to be followed, but can be a dynamic movement toward wholeness and health.

A final way in which the minister can help the process of grief is through preventative pastoral care. In a number of ways—for example, through education, exposing myths about death, and developing meaning in life—he can be several steps ahead of death, preparing his people and members of the community as a whole for handling it adaptively when it occurs.

NOTES

1. Gerald Caplan, *Principles of Preventative Psychiatry* (New York: Basic Books, 1963).

2. Ibid., p. 26.

3. Ibid., p. 113.

4. Gerald Gurin, Joseph Veroff, and Sheila Feld, *Americans View Their Mental Health* (New York: Basic Books, 1960), p. 307.

5. Edwin S. Shneidman and Philip Mandelkorn, "How to Prevent Suicide," (Washington, D.C.: Public Affairs Pamphlet #406).

6. Edgar Jackson, *Understanding Grief* (New York: Abingdon Press, 1957), p. 206.

7. Ibid., pp. 203–5.

8. Irene E. Clepper, quoted by Howard J. Clinebell, Jr., in *Basic Types of Pastoral Counseling* (New York: Abingdon Press, 1966), p. 187.

9. Ronald W. Maris, *Social Forces in Urban Suicide* (Homewood, Ill.: The Dorsey Press, 1969), p. 17.

10. Quoted in Joseph N. Bell, "Lifeline for Would-Be Suicides," reprinted from *Today's Health* (June, 1967): 3.

APPENDIX A
RESEARCH METHODOLOGY

Basic Hypothesis

This book is based on primary research recently completed by the author. The studies of Resnik, Cain and Fast, and others are also included to describe the effects of suicide on children and adolescents,[1] in order to give the reader a more complete picture of the suicide grief.

Inasmuch as *Suicide and Grief* is meant to be a practical guide to coping with the suicide grief and not a technical, scientific treatise, I wish to clarify a few aspects of the research methodology, without belaboring them.[2]

For research purposes one basic hypothesis was developed, along with a series of specific expectations which spelled out the hypothesis more clearly. The basic hypothesis was: *The pattern of the grief responses of suicide spouses will tend to be more disturbed (unadaptive) than the grief responses of non-suicide spouses.*

Specifically, the basic hypothesis proposed that the suicide survivors would feel more lonely and alienated from society, less involved in church, and would not hold their religious beliefs as strongly as non-suicide spouses; that they would not have as high an estimation of their marriage with the deceased (i.e., that it was not as intimate, not as "good" a marriage) as the non-suicide group; and that they would be more depressed and angry, feel more guilt, and have more suicide ideation and behavior than the non-suicide spouses. In general the suicide spouses would feel more restricted both inwardly and outwardly. To summarize, it was hypothesized that the suicide spouses would not adapt as well to the death of their marriage partners as would the non-suicide spouses.

Where, When, and with Whom

The research was carried out in Los Angeles County, California. Subjects were secured with the kind help of the Los Angeles Suicide Prevention Center and the Bureau of Records: Death Certificates, Los Angeles County.

Two groups of sixty individuals each were random-sampled out of the total population of their categories. Half (thirty) were male and half female in each of the two groups.

The criteria for the selection of both samples were as follows: (1) the deceased died in the same year so that all the griefs were from one to two years old; (2) the age of the deceased was between thirty and forty-nine years at the time of death; (3) the survivor was married and living with the deceased at the time of death, i.e., not separated or divorced; (4) no homicides or homicide-suicide combinations, or undecided classifications of deaths, were included. In summary, the members of this survey were early-middle and middle-aged Caucasian spouses who lived in Los Angeles County at the time of death. They were separated into two groups—those whose spouses died by suicide, and those whose spouses died by non-suicidal means.

The Grief Inventory

A paper and pencil test (the "Grief Inventory") was developed through a review of the literature in the area of suicide and grief, and through consultation with experts in the fields of ministry, psychological testing, suicide, and grief. It was pretested with subjects who fit within the previously mentioned criteria, but who had not been selected in the random sampling process.

The questionnaire was limited to four pages which included a series of demographic questions plus fifty-three Likert scale items. A Likert scale question is a statement (example: "I have been very depressed lately") with six possible responses, ranging from "agree very strongly" to "disagree very strongly." Three "lie" questions from the MMPI were included to determine if in either group there was a tendency toward a "halo" effect, i.e., if subjects of either group tried to portray themselves as being more healthy than they actually were. This did not occur.

When the pretesting was completed it was found that only individuals from fairly high income brackets and educational levels responded. Therefore, a $5.00 "token honorarium" was offered to each person who completed the inventory, hopefully to induce subjects from lower economic and educational levels to respond to the questionnaire.

Of the 120 subjects, 77.5% (93) were able to be personally contacted by the author. It is known that of the 27 who were not found, at least one (and it is believed two) had left the country. It is also possible that some of these 27 may have died since the death of the spouse. It is not known where the rest are presently residing or what they are doing.

Twenty-seven of the remaining 93 subjects refused to participate. Thus 55% of the total group, and 70.9% of those contacted, responded to the questionnaire—35 female and 31 male. This was considered a reasonably high percentage of positive response.

The Interviews

Of the 66 who responded to the questionnaire, several subjects were selected for intensive interviews of two to four hours' duration. The reason for the interviews was to get a fuller understanding of the different aspects of the grief response which were not necessarily contained in the grief inventory. No attempt was made to analyze statistically the data gleaned from the interviews.

There was no random method of selecting the subjects of the interviews. The bases for selection were: (1) all individuals selected had indicated on the last question of the Grief Inventory that they would be willing to talk further with the author; (2) some were selected who evidenced suicidal ideation and some who did not; (3) subjects were selected from different income and educational levels; and (4) some were selected who were religious, and others who were not.

The method of interviewing was nondirective. An interview schedule was used very loosely during the interviews, and all interviews were taped and later transcribed.

How the Data Was Evaluated

The responses to the Grief Inventory were punched on IBM cards, and an IBM 360 computer was used to perform the statistical computations. Several statistical tests were implemented to evaluate the data and to determine if there was a statistical difference between the grief responses of the two groups (suicide and non-suicide). The generally accepted level of significant difference (greater than .05) was used.

NOTES

1. See the Annotated Bibliography.
2. The reader who desires more specific information on the research methodology or the complete statistical results is referred to Howard W. Stone, "The Grief Responses of Middle-Aged Spouses: Suicide and Non-Suicide Compared" (Th.D. dissertation, School of Theology at Claremont, Claremont, California, 1971). Copy may be obtained from the University Microfilms, P.O. Box 1346, Ann Arbor, Michigan 48106.

APPENDIX B
RESULTS OF THE SURVEY

This appendix includes some of the statistical results of the grief inventory. The first part gives basic background (demographic) information. The second part of the appendix lists the 53 Likert scale items. Listed beside the title of each of these questions is the value of Chi Square comparing the total number of those who agreed with the number of those who disagreed. Asterisked items indicate a significant difference between the suicide and non-suicide survivors' responses to the question. The double asterisk indicates a significance of greater than .01. The single asterisk indicates a significance of greater than .05.

I. BACKGROUND INFORMATION (DEMOGRAPHIC DATA)

1. Age:	Suicide	Non-Suicide	Total
25-29		1	1
30-34	2	3	5
35-39	9	4	13
40-44	7	6	13
45-49	10	11	21
50-54	3	3	6
55-59	3	1	4
60-64	1	2	3
Total	35	31	66

High age:
    Suicide: 62
    Non-suicide: 66
Low age:
    Suicide: 31
    Non-suicide: 27

Means:

Suicide male:	46.5	Non-suicide male:	48.1
Suicide female:	42.4	Non-suicide female:	40.8
Total:	44.3	Total:	44.3

2. Present marital status
since death of spouse:

	Suicide	Non-Suicide	Total
Engaged	2	1	3
Remarried	7	7	14
Remarried & separated	1	1	2
Remarried & divorced		1	1
Widowed	25	21	46

3. Education:

	Suicide	Non-Suicide	Total
Up to 8th grade		1	1
8th to 12th grade	16	14	30
Some college	19	16	35

4. How long had you been married
at the time of death?

	Suicide	Non-Suicide	Total
0- 5 years	8	3	11
6-10 years	4	3	7
11-15 years	5	4	9
16-20 years	5	6	11
21-25 years	9	12	21
26-30 years	4	3	7

Means:

Suicide male:	16.0	Non-suicide male:	19.6
Suicide female:	14.7	Non-suicide female:	17.1
Total:	15.3	Total:	18.3

5. Have you moved since your
spouse died?

	Suicide	Non-Suicide	Total
Yes	11	10	21
No	24	21	45

6. Cause of spouse's death:

Accident:	3
Illness:	28
Suicide:	35

Sudden deaths: 11 (non-sucide)
Non-sudden deaths: 20 (non-suicide)

7. Organizations and clubs:

	Suicide	Non-Suicide	Total
Belong to	20	18	38
Attend regularly	8	13	21
Contribute financially	18	17	35
Belong to committee	2	5	7
Hold an office		2	2

8. Annual income:

	Suicide	Non-Suicide	Total
to $2999	2	3	5
$3000-5999	8	8	16
$6000-8999	4	4	8
$9000-11,999	4	7	11
$12,000-14,999	6	3	9
$15,000 plus	9	4	13
No answer	2	2	4

9. Religious affiliation:

	Suicide	Non-Suicide	Total
Protestant	20	18	38
Roman Catholic	6	7	13
Orthodox Church			
Jewish	6	1	7
Other		1	1
None	3	4	7

10. How often do you attend church:

	Suicide	Non-Suicide	Total
Just about every week	5	5	10
Once a month or more	4	4	8
Several times a year	15	15	30
Never	11	7	18

II. LIKERT SCALE ITEMS

Please answer the following questions honestly, stating how you have felt *since* the death of your spouse.	S or N	Agree very much 1	Agree pretty much 2	Agree a little 3	Disagree a little 4	Disagree pretty much 5	Disagree very much 6	No answer N	Question does not apply ✓	Total of all who agree 1-3	Total of all who disagree 4-6
1. *Sickness:* 11.85** I have not been as healthy since the death of my spouse (i.e. asthma, rheumatism, colds, rashes, headaches, etc.).	S	7	4	8	3	2	11			19	16
	N		1	3	2	5	19	1		4	26
2. *Finances:* 1.71 I have gotten along all right financially since the death of my spouse.	S	13	10	3	2	5	2			26	9
	N	17	9	1	1	1	2			27	4
3. *Meaning of religion:* 2.38 I believe I have been more religious since the death of my spouse.	S	4	4	7	3	4	12	1		15	19
	N	2	4	2	7	3	13			8	23
4. *Importance of the church:* 3.48 My church has not been of very much help to me in the hard times since my husband/wife died.	S	11	4	7	2		9	2		22	11
	N	8	3	1	3	6	7	3		12	16
5. *Quality of marriage at time of death:* 6.63* Our marriage at the time of death was going "downhill."	S	7	4	5		3	16			16	19
	N	1	2	2	1		25			5	26

117

	S or N	1	2	3	4	5	6	N	✓	1-3	4-6

6. *Funeral:* 0.40
I feel the funeral helped me greatly at the time of his/her death.

| | S | 4 | 5 | 3 | 3 | 4 | 14 | 2 | | 12 | 21 |
| | N | 2 | 4 | 6 | 2 | 3 | 10 | 4 | | 12 | 15 |

7. *Stigma of suicide:* 6.69**
At times I have felt like I was being compelled to move residence because of what some people thought about my spouse dying.

| | S | 4 | | 5 | | | 26 | | | 9 | 26 |
| | N | | | | | | 29 | 2 | | 0 | 29 |

8. *Need of therapeutic intervention:* 0.55
I have felt like I (and/or my children) have needed counseling since the death of my spouse.

| | S | 7 | 4 | 3 | 3 | 5 | 12 | 1 | | 14 | 20 |
| | N | 3 | 4 | 3 | | 2 | 19 | | | 10 | 21 |

Have you had counseling?
(Yes: S: 10, N: 3)
Had you ever had counseling before your spouse died?
(Yes: S: 12, N: 2)

9. *Problems in raising children:* 0.02
My children have been more difficult to raise since my spouse's death. (Check if no children living with you at time of death.)

| | S | 6 | 1 | 6 | 1 | | 12 | | 9 | 13 | 13 |
| | N | 4 | 4 | 4 | 1 | 2 | 8 | 1 | 7 | 12 | 11 |

10. *Social withdrawal:* 0.03
Friends and relatives don't seem as close to me as they did before my spouse died.

| | S | 6 | 1 | 5 | 2 | 2 | 18 | 1 | | 12 | 22 |
| | N | 6 | 3 | 1 | | | 6 | 14 | 1 | 10 | 20 |

	S or N	1	2	3	4	5	6	N ✔	1-3	4-6
11. Religious solace: 0.02 The death of my spouse has made me turn to God for help.	S	10	1	6	3	5	10		17	18
	N	4	3	7			1	15	1	14	16
12. Quality of marriage at time of death: 4.36* I don't completely understand why, but in the last few months before the death of my spouse, we argued and verbally fought a lot.	S	4	3	5	1	4	18		12	23
	N		2	1	2	2	24		3	28
13. Meaning in life: 0.05 Since my spouse died I have not had anything to live for.	S	1		3		7	24		4	31
	N	1	2	1	2	1	23	1	4	26
14. Social involvement: 0.76 I now feel left out of social life more than I used to be.	S	5	3	2	4	6	15		10	25
	N		6	6	2	2	15		12	19
15. Quality of marriage intimacy: 0.04 My spouse hardly ever confided in me.	S	2	2	1	6	5	19		5	30
	N	2	2	1			3	23		5	26
16. Perceived blaming of friends and relatives: 5.15* I have felt blamed by others to some extent for my spouse's death.	S	1		8		5	21		9	26
	N			1		1	29		1	30

	S or N	1	2	3	4	5	6	N	✓	1-3	4-6
17. *Drinking:* 1.49 I am drinking more alcoholic beverages than before the death. (Check if never have drunk.)	S	2	4	6		1	16		6	12	17
	N	2		5	1	3	16		4	7	20
18. *Anger at spouse:* 6.92** There have been times since he/she died that I have felt mildly irritated or disappointed in him/her.	S	7	2	10	2	4	10			19	16
	N	1	2	4	1	1	22			7	24
19. *Anger:* 0.78 Since my spouse died I get annoyed or irritated more easily than I used to.	S	3	1	11	2	10	8			15	20
	N	4	1	5	1	7	13			10	21
20. *Loneliness:* 1.95 I am a more lonely person since the death of my spouse.	S	13	8	5	2	1	6			26	9
	N	8	6	4	3	1	9			18	13
21. *Use of drugs:* 0.38 Since the death of my spouse I have been using more drugs (such as tranquilizers, sleeping pills, narcotics, pep pills, etc.).	S	1	1	3		2	27	1		5	29
	N	2	1				28			3	28
22. *Feeling about future:* 2.24 I am not as confident about the future as I was before the death of my spouse.	S	7	6	7		2	13			20	15
	N	5		7	3	2	14			12	19
23. *Crying:* 3.55 I have not cried to speak of since my spouse died.	S	3	2		5	6	19			5	30
	N	6	1	4	2	4	12	2		11	18

Appendix B: Results of the Survey

Resources

Circle any of the following which were very helpful in aiding you to adjust to your spouse's death.	Suicide	Non-Suicide	Total
Yourself	24	19	43
Minister/rabbi/priest	6	8	14
Parental family	15	10	25
Other relatives	11	10	21
Your children	23	19	42
Counselor/psychotherapist	2		2
Friends	26	19	45
Prayer, reading the Bible	11	7	18
Church	8	4	12
Family doctor	6	5	11
Social worker	2		2
Other professionals	1	2	3
Funeral	4	2	6
No one	3		3
Other	4	6	10

Suicidal Behavior and Ideation

Circle any of the following which express your feelings since the death of your husband or wife. Mark "B" in front of the sentence which expresses your feelings *before* the death.

	Circled		"B"	
	S	N	S	N
Not thought about killing myself at all.	19	22	14	15
Thought only a little about killing myself, but not for quite a while.	3	1	4	1
Thought about killing myself off and on.	4		1	
Thought about killing myself fairly often but have not told anybody.	1	1		
Thought a lot about it and told others I felt like killing myself.		1		
Attempted suicide.	1			
No answer.	7	6	16	15

121

Please answer the following questions as to how you feel *now*.	S or N	1	2	3	4	5	6	N ✔	1-3	4-6
24. *Dependency vs. Independency*: 0.65 I feel independent now, not needing to depend on others.	S	8	10		2	7	8		18	17
	N	9	7	3	2	6	4		19	12
25. *Importance of Religion*: 0.23 I can take religion or leave it.	S	9	4	3	4	8	7		16	19
	N	5	5	6	2	5	8		16	15
26. *Prayer*: 1.36 Prayer can solve many problems.	S	11	1	8	3	4	8		20	15
	N	10	7	5			9		22	9
27. *Lie*: 3.71 Once in a while I put off until tomorrow what I ought to do today.	S	10	11	12	1	1			33	2
	N	7	5	11	3	1	4		23	8
28. *God's Providence*: 0.48 God protects from harm all those who really trust in him.	S	8	5	5	2	8	7		18	17
	N	10	4	4	2	2	8	1	18	12
29. *Beliefs on suicide*: 0.07 Nothing is worth killing yourself for.	S	21	7	2	1	1	2	1	30	4
	N	27		1	1	1	1		28	3
30. *Depression*: 0.03 It does not take me long to get over feeling gloomy.	S	10	9	5	4	2	5		24	11
	N	10	10	3	4	3	1		23	8
31. *Perceived Social Respect*: 0.77 I am looked upon as being of small or no account in other people's eyes.	S			3	1	11	20		3	32
	N			1	1	3	25	1	1	29

	S or N	1	2	3	4	5	6	N ✔	1-3	4-6

32. Lie: 0.33
Sometimes when I am not feeling well I am cross.

	S or N	1	2	3	4	5	6	N ✔	1-3	4-6
	S	10	10	12	1	2			32	3
	N	11	3	13	1	2	1		27	4

33. Feeling of freedom (personal) and social constraint: 0.31
I feel trapped, oppressed, forced to do things I don't want to do.

	S or N	1	2	3	4	5	6	N ✔	1-3	4-6
	S	2	2	6	5	10	10		10	25
	N		4	3		4	20		7	24

34. Work: 1.13
I get a great deal of satisfaction out of my work (Check if you have not worked full or part time since your spouse died).

	S or N	1	2	3	4	5	6	N ✔	1-3	4-6
	S	14	9	2	2	3		5	25	5
	N	18	5	2			2	4	25	2

35. Anxiety or Calmness: 0.62
I feel pretty generally secure and free from care.

	S or N	1	2	3	4	5	6	N ✔	1-3	4-6
	S	4	10	6	4	5	6		20	15
	N	10	7	3	6	2	2	1	20	10

36. Belief on suicide: 0.31
Suicide is morally wrong.

	S or N	1	2	3	4	5	6	N ✔	1-3	4-6
	S	19	2	4	1	4	5		25	10
	N	22	1	1	2	1	4		24	7

37. Acceptance of the Loss: 0.04
I still have trouble realizing that my spouse is dead.

	S or N	1	2	3	4	5	6	N ✔	1-3	4-6
	S	10	5	5	1	3	11		20	15
	N	7	3	7	1	2	11		17	14

38. Impulsiveness vs. Self-restraint: 0.01
I refuse to allow myself the slightest self-indulgence or impulsive action.

	S or N	1	2	3	4	5	6	N ✔	1-3	4-6
	S	3	2	5	6	9	10		10	25
	N	2	3	3	6	8	7	2	8	21

	S or N	1	2	3	4	5	6	N	✔	1-3	4-6

39. *Sleep Disturbance:* 0.01
I have some trouble sleeping and wake up more tired in the morning than I used to.

	S	4	2	8		8	13			14	21
	N	3	6	3	1		18			12	19

40. *Fatigue:* 3.41
I feel physically tired much of the time.

	S	4	8	6	2	2	13			18	17
	N	4	2	3	2	4	16			9	22

41. *Punishment:* 2.84
At times I feel I deserve to be punished.

	S			9		7	19			9	26
	N		1	2		6	22			3	28

42. *Depression:* 0.28
I feel depressed and very low and miserable most of the time.

	S		1	2	4	9	18	1		3	31
	N		2	2	1	5	21			4	27

43. *Reaction to Consolation:* 0.00
After a while I got tired of people always trying to console me about my spouse's death.

	S	4	3	6	4	2	14	2		13	20
	N	4	3	5	2	5	12			12	19

44. *Guilt:* 8.68**
I feel guilty about some things I said and did before my spouse died.

	S	4	5	15		5	6			24	11
	N	2	3	5	1	5	15			10	21

45. *Openness with Feelings:* 0.04
I fear to express my deepest feelings to other people, even those close to me.

	S	4	3	4	2	9	13			11	24
	N	2	4	3	4	3	15			9	22

	S or N	1	2	3	4	5	6	N	✔	1-3	4-6
46. *Guilt:* 5.54* I often think I should have done more for my spouse before he/she died.	S	7	7	8	1	6	5	1		22	12
	N	2	3	6	1	3	16			11	20
47. *Guilt:* 13.88** Although I feel I maybe shouldn't, at times I feel ashamed about the way my husband/wife died.	S	7	3	8	1	3	12	1		18	16
	N			3	1	2	25			3	28
48. *Scape-Goating:* 0.23 If it weren't for my spouse, I'd be in a lot better shape today in this world.	S	1		1	5	4	23	1		2	32
	N			1	2	3	24	1		1	29
49. *Stalemated grief reaction:* 0.29 I just can't seem to get over the death of my spouse.	S	7	4	6		6	12			17	18
	N	2	4	7	1	3	14			13	18
50. *Guilt:* 6.20* Although I don't like to think of it, I feel at times as if I were part of the cause of my spouse's death.	S	1	4	10	2	3	14	1		15	19
	N			4	1	2	24			4	27
51. *Self-confidence or feeling of inadequacy:* 0.03 I am distressed by my weakness and lack of ability, sick of my incompetence.	S	2		2	1	3	27			4	31
	N	1	1	2		4	23			4	27

	S or N	1	2	3	4	5	6	N ✓	1-3	4-6
52. *Lie:* 0.03										
I do not like everyone I know.	S	6	5	10	2	4	8		21	14
	N	8	2	8	2	4	7		18	13
53. *Avoidance of lost object:* 0.11										
I try to avoid anything that reminds me of my spouse.	S	1	1	1	2	7	23		3	32
	N		2		1	6	22		2	29

GLOSSARY

Suicide. The definition of suicide offered by Shneidman is quoted:

As a beginning, a straightforward definition of suicide might read: "Suicide is the human act of self-inflicted, self-intentioned cessation." At least five points are to be noted in this brief definition: (1) it states that suicide is a human act; (2) it combines both the decedent's conscious wish to be dead and his actions to carry out that wish; (3) it implies that the motivations of the deceased may have to be inferred and his behaviors interpreted by others, using such evidence as a suicide note, spoken testimony, or retrospective reconstruction of the victim's intentions; (4) it states that the goal of the action relates to death, rather than to self-injury, self-mutilation, inimical or self-reducing behaviors; and (5) it focuses on the concept of cessation—the final stopping or naughtment of the individual's conscious introspective life.[1]

It might be noted that, unless stated otherwise, this book refers to those who have completed the act of suicide, not those who are threatening to, or who have attempted to take their lives. The term *suicidal* will be applied rather indiscriminately to all people who it is determined have definite tendencies toward killing themselves in the near future.

Grief reaction. This term refers to the psychological response of a mourning person to the loss of a loved one by death. There are two important sides of this definition: one, it is a *loss;* and two, the person lost is a *love* (or need-satisfying) *object.* It amounts to the way the survivors reorient their lives without the deceased. The seven phases of the grief reaction, which have been developed by the author, are included in Chapter 3.

Adaptive and unadaptive grief. An unadaptive grief reaction is the psychological response of the bereaved which is considerably more disturbed than normal. This disturbed grief reaction is frequently manifested by one characteristic of the phases of grief becoming blocked (e.g., constant crying, or guilt, or continual festering hostility). The result is an unresolved grief which the individual is not able to work through. An adaptive grief reaction is a "normal," healthy response to the loss of a loved one. It involves an individual adequately resolving the different dynamics of grief without becoming "stuck" in any one of them.

Grief response. The term as used in this book has a more general meaning than grief reaction. The latter refers to the psychological response to the loss; whereas grief response indicates not only the emotional aspects of the grief reaction, but also how the survivor reacts financially, what resources he uses, his church attendance (or lack of it), his changing religious beliefs, his work record, etc. In other words, it includes the behavioral and social changes he makes in response to his grief as well as the emotional ones. The major focus of the research behind this book is the broader grief response and not just the grief reaction.

Resources. The use of this term indicates those persons ("significant others"), institutions, or organizations upon which an individual might draw for help and solace in times of grief. Using the resources available to him would tend to help a person work through the grief more adaptively.

Dynamics (psychodynamics) of grief. This will refer to the natural course the grief reaction generally follows—the pattern or configuration of the different emotional elements of the grief reaction.

Crisis. This term indicates an individual's internal reaction to a perceived external hazard (e.g., death of a loved one, divorce, loss of job, etc.). The three conditions which constitute a crisis, as indicated by Caplan, are (1) a severe precipitating stress; (2) extensive emotional arousal; and (3) the pressure to resolve the dissonance caused by the stress and return to homeostasis.[2]

Crisis intervention. Crisis intervention (sometimes referred to only as intervention) indicates the relatively new method of aiding people in coping with emotionally decisive moments in their lives (crises). It includes counseling and other activities designed to influence the course of a particular crisis so that an adaptive way of behaving and relating will result, including the ability to better cope with future crises.

Preventative pastoral care. This includes any activity of the pastor or his parishioners which aims at (1) reducing the incidence of pastoral care and counseling problems among his parishioners; (2) reducing the duration of such problems; (3) reducing the residual impairment caused by these problems. Preventative pastoral care can involve activities which focus on controlling mental health problems, such as: pastoral counseling, Christian education, family life education, the use of sharing groups, and the like.

NOTES

1. Edwin S. Shneidman, "Suicidal Phenomena: Their Definition and Classification" (Los Angeles: Suicide Prevention Center, mimeographed and published n.d.).

2. Gerald Caplan, *Principles of Preventive Psychiatry* (New York: Basic Books, Inc., 1964), pp. 39–41.

ANNOTATED BIBLIOGRAPHY

GENERAL INFORMATION ON GRIEF

Clayton, Paula, Lynn Desmarais, and George Winokur. "A Study of Normal Bereavement." *American Journal of Psychiatry* CXXV: 2 (1968): 168–78.
This article is valuable because the research was on "normal" rather than "pathological" groups of individuals, and also because it is an attempt at empirical valuation of the grief.

Irion, Paul E. *The Funeral and the Mourners.* New York: Abingdon Press, 1954.
Although I do not agree with all Irion has to say about the funeral, I find this book helpful on the subject.

Jackson, Edgar N. *Understanding Grief.* New York: Abingdon Press, 1957.
Jackson has written several books on grief, and I believe this is his most valuable one.

Lindemann, Erich. "Symptomatology and Management of Acute Grief." *Pastoral Psychology* XIV:36 (September, 1963): 8–18.
This is a reprint of Lindemann's classic article on grief referred to in Chapter 2 of this book.

Marris, P. *Widows and Their Families.* London: Routledge & Kegan Paul, 1958.
Marris studied the aftermath of the loss of a husband by death in English widows. The book includes some interesting demographic statistical findings.

Switzer, David K. *The Dynamics of Grief.* New York: Abingdon Press, 1970.
Switzer believes the basic dynamic of all grief is anxiety.

Westberg, Granger F. *Good Grief.* Philadelphia: Fortress Press, 1962.
A short book (fifty-seven pages) describing what Westberg believes to be the ten stages of grief.

Annotated Bibliography

General Information on Suicide

Clinebell, Howard J., Jr. "The Suicidal Emergency." *First Aid in Counseling*. Edited by C. L. Mitton. Edinburgh: T. & T. Clark, 1968.
Chapter 14 of this book includes the description by Clinebell, a pastoral counselor, on how he believes the suicide crisis should be handled.

Farberow, Norman L. *Bibliography on Suicide and Suicide Prevention*. Washington, D.C.: National Clearinghouse for Mental Health Information, Public Health Services Publication No. 1979, 1969.
A very complete bibliography on all phases of suicide.

Farberow, Norman L. and Edwin S. Shneidman, eds. *The Cry For Help*. New York: McGraw-Hill, 1965.
Includes much information about suicide by various authors. Especially helpful are Chapters 12 through 20, which include the ways seven different psychotherapeutic schools view the dynamics of suicide.

Farberow, Norman L., Samuel M. Heilig, and Robert E. Litman. *Techniques in Crisis Intervention: A Training Manual*. Los Angeles: Suicide Prevention Center, Inc., 1968.
Most valuable guide to counseling an individual who is considering suicide. Short and yet very helpful.

Resnik, H. L. P., ed. *Suicidal Behaviors*. Boston: Little Brown & Co., 1968.
This volume includes thirty-eight generally excellent articles on all phases of the diagnosis and management of suicide.

Suicide Grief

Cain, Albert C. and Irene Fast. "Children's Disturbed Reactions to Parent Suicide." *American Journal of Orthopsychiatry* XXXVI:5 (1966): 873–80.
"A Clinical Study of Some Aspects of the Psychological Importance of Parent Suicide Upon Children." *American Journal of Orthopsychiatry* XXXV:2 (1965): 318–19.
"The Legacy of Suicide: Observations on the Pathogenic Impact of Suicide Upon Marital Partners." *Psychiatry* XXIX:4 (1966): 406–11.
These three articles describe the work and research of Cain and Fast with the children of parents who committed suicide. The third article also describes how the authors quite incidentally discovered pathological patterns of behavior in the surviving marriage partner while studying the children.

Herzog, Alfred, and H. L. P. Resnik. "A Clinical Study of Parental Response to Adolescent Death by Suicide with Recommendations for Approaching the Survivors." *Suicide and its Prevention: Proceedings of the Fourth International Conference for Suicide Prevention.* Edited by Norman L. Farberow. Los Angeles: Delmar Publishing Co., 1968. Pp. 381–90.

Herzog and Resnik found frequent family disruption among parents of an adolescent suicide.

Lindemann, Erich. "A Study of Grief: Emotional Responses to Suicide." *Pastoral Psychology* IV (1953): 9–13.

In this article Lindemann indicates that suicide survivors are likely to get "stuck" in their grief and for years be in a state of cold isolation.

CRISIS INTERVENTION COUNSELING

Caplan, Gerald. *Principles of Preventive Psychiatry.* New York: Basic Books, 1964.

In Caplan's second chapter, "A Conceptual Model for Primary Prevention," he describes the characteristics of significant life crises and factors which influence their outcome.

Clinebell, Howard J., Jr. *Basic Types of Pastoral Counseling.* New York: Abingdon Press, 1966.

Chapter 9 of this valuable book is on crisis counseling. Clinebell suggests several different approaches to crisis counseling.

Parad, Howard J. *Crisis Intervention: Selected Readings.* New York: Family Service Association of America, 1965.

This book includes twenty-nine chapters of varying quality. Two of the more valuable ones are Lindemann's classic article on grief and Hill's chapter on crisis in the family.

Pastoral Psychology XXI:203 (April, 1970).

The entire issue of this journal is devoted to the minister and crisis counseling.

Pretzel, Paul W. "An Introduction to Crisis Counseling: Making the Best Use of the Dangerous Opportunity." *Research and Pupil Personnel Services Newsletter* VII:3 (March 13, 1970): Los Angeles School System, 4–6.

A short, clear and concise description of what crisis intervention counseling is, written for non-mental health professionals.

Taplin, Julian R. "Crisis Theory: Critique and Reformulation." *Community Mental Health Journal* VII:1 (1971): 13–23.

A good attempt at reformulating crisis theory in less psychoanalytic constructs. Presents eight basic aspects that occur in a crisis.

INDEX